Performing Shakespeare

A Guidebook

J. W. Aykroyd

A Samuel French Acting Edition

FOUNDED 1830

SAMUELFRENCH-LONDON.CO.UK
SAMUELFRENCH.COM

Copyright © 1979 by J. W. Aykroyd
All Rights Reserved

PERFORMING SHAKESPEARE is fully protected under the copyright laws of the British Commonwealth, including Canada, the United States of America, and all other countries of the Copyright Union. All rights, including professional and amateur stage productions, recitation, lecturing, public reading, motion picture, radio broadcasting, television and the rights of translation into foreign languages are strictly reserved.

ISBN 978-0-573-09035-6

www.samuelfrench-london.co.uk

www.samuelfrench.com

FOR AMATEUR PRODUCTION ENQUIRIES

UNITED KINGDOM AND WORLD EXCLUDING NORTH AMERICA

plays@SamuelFrench-London.co.uk

020 7255 4302/01

Each title is subject to availability from Samuel French, depending upon country of performance.

CAUTION: Professional and amateur producers are hereby warned that *PERFORMING SHAKESPEARE* is subject to a licensing fee. Publication of this play does not imply availability for performance. Both amateurs and professionals considering a production are strongly advised to apply to the appropriate agent before starting rehearsals, advertising, or booking a theatre. A licensing fee must be paid whether the title is presented for charity or gain and whether or not admission is charged.

The professional rights in this play are controlled by Sheil Land Associates, 52 Doughty Street, London, WC1N 2LS.

No one shall make any changes in this title for the purpose of production. No part of this book may be reproduced, stored in a retrieval system, or transmitted in any form, by any means, now known or yet to be invented, including mechanical, electronic, photocopying, recording, videotaping, or otherwise, without the prior written permission of the publisher. No one shall upload this title, or part of this title, to any social media websites.

The right of J. W. Aykroyd to be identified as author of this work has been asserted by him in accordance with Section 77 of the Copyright, Designs and Patents Act 1988

Contents

	PREFACE	v
CHAPTER 1	CHOOSING THE PLAY	1
CHAPTER 2	PREPARING THE TEXT	5
CHAPTER 3	STAGING SHAKESPEARE	20
CHAPTER 4	ACTING SHAKESPEARE	36
CHAPTER 5	SPEAKING THE TEXT	55
CHAPTER 6	FIGHTS AND BATTLES	64
CHAPTER 7	COSTUMES AND PROPS	73
CHAPTER 8	MUSIC AND DANCING	87
CHAPTER 9	PERFORMERS' GUIDE TO THE PLAYS	93
	APPENDIX: Voice Exercises	115

Abbreviations used for the titles of Shakespeare's Plays

All's Well	All's Well that Ends Well
Ant & Cl	Antony and Cleopatra
AYL	As You Like It
Com Err	The Comedy of Errors
Cor	Coriolanus
Cymb	Cymbeline
Ham	Hamlet
1 Hen IV	King Henry IV Part 1
2 Hen IV	King Henry IV Part 2
Hen V	The Life of King Henry V
1 Hen VI	King Henry VI Part 1
2 Hen VI	King Henry VI Part 2
3 Hen VI	King Henry VI Part 3
Hen VIII	The Famous History of the Life of King Henry VIII
John	The Life and Death of King John
Jul C	Julius Caesar
Lear	King Lear
LLL	Love's Labour's Lost
Macb	Macbeth
Meas for M	Measure for Measure
Merch V	The Merchant of Venice
Merry W	The Merry Wives of Windsor
Mids N	A Midsummer-Night's Dream
Much Ado	Much Ado about Nothing
Oth	Othello, the Moor of Venice
Per	Pericles
Rich II	The Tragedy of King Richard II
Rich III	The Tragedy of King Richard III
Rom & Jul	Romeo and Juliet
Tam Shr	The Taming of the Shrew
Temp	The Tempest
Timon	Timon of Athens
Tit A	Titus Andronicus
Tr & Cr	Troilus and Cressida
Twel N	Twelfth Night
Two Gent	The Two Gentlemen of Verona
Wint T	The Winter's Tale

Preface

It is hoped that the information collected in this book will be of use to English teachers and drama groups in schools and colleges, to student actors and to local amateur societies. Aspects of staging, acting, music, clothes, props and furniture which are relevant to Shakespeare production are outlined; suppliers, sources and books for further reading are listed, and a short account of each play in terms of minimum and maximum casting, basic props and effects is given in Chapter 9. Versions and possible extracts are suggested for groups who do not have scope for a full-scale production.

The plays are approached, as they were written, as blueprints for performance. Chapters 3, 4 and 5 show how the text contains implicit and explicit directions to the performers. Exploring these directions and putting them into practice in a way that Shakespeare's own actors might have done is by far the most interesting and rewarding way for young people to learn about Shakespeare.

The book is addressed to the Performer: an imaginary Hercules, with responsibility for directing, acting, wardrobe, stagemanagement, music, props and everything else. Quite often in amateur groups one person does indeed cope with all these things. Otherwise, all departments should of course be in blissful creative accord.

Some of the books suggested for further reading are now out of print but are of course available in reference libraries.

I am grateful to Timothy Hilton, Martin Best, Robert Spencer, Nicholas Lacey, Gillian Somerville-Large and my parents for their kind help and encouragement in the preparation of this book.

All Shakespeare quotations (other than those from the First Folio) are from the OUP edition by W J Craig (1905) of the Complete Works. Abbreviated play titles are according to the *OED*. A list of these is given opposite.

1 Choosing the Play

GENERAL POINTS

Your first consideration in choosing your play is whether it is right for the cast. Don't worry about the audience at this point. Some will probably turn up to watch dutifully, expecting a heavy evening. It's your business to astonish and enrapture them. But if your cast is bored or baffled by the play, the production doesn't stand a chance.

CASTING

The plays provide a lot of leeway for whatever numbers and talents are at your disposal. If you are short of actors remember that many parts were probably intended for doubling (see Chapter 9), or you can do scenes (see below, p. 3). Boys can play girls, as at the Elizabethan playhouses, and girls can quite easily play boys. Alternatively, if you have a large cast, numberless jobs can be created for mobs, spear carriers, attendant lords, etc. It is usually a good idea to centre your choice on your best actors.

TRAGEDY OR COMEDY?

It is a mistake to think that a mild comedy like *Much Ado* will go down better with a village-hall audience than, for example, *Titus Andronicus*. This is not necessarily so at all. The comedies are often thought of as suitable or entertaining because they are 'light'; but they are not easy to perform. Romantic comedies especially (*LLL, Two Gent, Twel N, Much Ado, AYL, Merch V*) are complicated tapestries of wit, melancholy and sexuality. Much of their activity is verbal rather than visible. They need to be acted with huge energy; otherwise they can be flat and depressing. An inexperienced cast would be safer with an early bourgeois comedy (*Merry W, Com Err, Tam Shr*). These work well if done with exuberance and lots of inventive slapstick.

Young people tend to enjoy blood, sex and battles, and Shakespeare offers plenty of all three (*Rom & Jul, John*, the *Henrys, Rich III, Tr & Cr, Per, Ant & Cl, Tit A*). If you decide to do a heroic tragedy (*Rich II, Macb, Ham, Timon, Lear, Oth*) don't fall into the trap of thinking of it as entirely gloomy. Explore and exploit all the comic counter-tragic material that Shakespeare provides. Also, make sure you have the *right* actor/actress for the leading parts. This may sound absurdly obvious, but it is the crux of the production. A good actor will not necessarily be a good Othello, but if Othello is unbelievable or uninteresting your production won't get off the ground.

ACTION

Very broadly speaking, people of all ages will tend to be more interested in what they see—which is easy—than in the words—which are archaic and difficult. If you have reason to believe that your audience is not particularly addicted to the Bard, think about the physical action of the plays within your scope, and decide which one you can make the most exciting to watch. The *Henry VI*s, *John, Per, Rom & Jul, Macb, 1 Hen IV, Hen V, Merry W, Mids N, Temp* and *Tam Shr* are rich in visual action of a readily understandable kind, and you can always trim the discoursive scenes. Don't be daunted by battles; they are tests of directorial ingenuity (see Chapter 6).

The narrative romances, *Cymb, Meas for M, All's Well, Wint T, Tr & Cr*, and *Per*, need to be performed with vitality and intelligence, especially *Meas for M, Tr & Cr* and *All's Well*, with their gloomy intellectuality and ambiguous endings. Perhaps these work best with mature casts.

FAMILIARITY

If you decide on a lesser-known play, remember that it is lesser known because it has theatrical weaknesses. Decide what they are and allow for them. On the other hand, if you decide to do a chestnut like *Twelfth Night*, remember that while many people will never have seen it before, those that have will have high expectations of the production. Don't assume that a good, well-tried play will stand up to a slapdash performance.

Whichever play you choose, pretend you have just discovered the script in a secret drawer and are mounting the first-ever production.

AMENITIES

Your last and least problem is space and scenery. Shakespeare constructed most of his plays for mobility and they can be performed pretty well anywhere, with minimal sets, props and basic lighting (see Chapter 3).

CROSS-SECTIONS

If a full-scale production is beyond your scope, you could do a cross-section of scenes from one play or several plays. Try to give each chunk a coherent shape and a climax. Think of it as a sort of film trailer; your intention is to make the audience want to see the whole play. For example, you could do a version of *The Tempest* like this:

Enter Narrator; describes, crisply, the situation of Prospero and his household, and the shipwreck of Alonso and company. Concludes by saying: 'Among the shipwrecked survivors is Alonso's son, Ferdinand.' Appropriate music, noises, etc. Enter Ariel, singing 'Come unto these yellow sands.' Proceed from Act 1 scene 2, line 401 straight through 2.1 (you might cut lines 76–112 and 131–47), 2.2, 3.1 to the end of 3.2.

Other possibilities are:

Twelfth Night, or *The Fortunes of Viola*: Act 1, scenes 2, 4 and 5 starting the latter at line 106; followed by 2.2, 2.4, 3.1 and 3.4, starting the latter at line 224 and ending at 421: '. . . fresh in love.'

Or: *Julius Caesar*, or *The Tyrant's Death*. 1.2, 1.3, 2.1, 2.2, 3.2, ending at line 118: '. . . The men that gave their country liberty.' If you are stuck for ideas for cross-sections, the British Drama League Library (British Theatre Association, 9 Fitzroy Square, London W1P 6AE) can supply shortened versions which range between a few minutes and over an hour.

ANTHOLOGIES

The plays can also be mined for anthologies, or programmes of speeches and scenes which illustrate a particular Shakespearian theme. They can be laced with songs, music and dances. Again, they must be designed carefully to involve the audience's emotions. Don't be satisfied with a dull series of extracts.

Suppose you wanted to compile a programme on Shakespeare's treatment of madness. You would begin by giving it an enticing title. Theseus's speech, 'Lovers and madmen have such seething brains', (*Mids N* 5.1.4) could start you off. You could string together the schizophrenics, such as Cassandra (*Tr & Cr*) and Ophelia, with the feigned madmen, Hamlet (3.1 or 3.2) and Edgar (*Lear* 3.4). You could illustrate the breakdown of the mind with Lady Macbeth sleepwalking or Lear (3.4 or 4.2). You might include the sinister Sir Topas scene (*Twel N* 4.2) to show how close to madness are the satanic, fragmentary minds of Shakespeare's sardonic fools. You might conclude with some scenes where fantasy sails dangerously close to the dream-world that everyone shares: the *Tam Shr* Induction, Sebastian's speech (*Twel N* 4.1) 'This is the air . . .', and Bottom's waking speech (*Mids N* 4.1). You could end romantically with Ophelia and her songs, *Ham* 4.5, to line 200: 'God be wi' ye!'

Other possible themes: *War and Peace, Women in Love, Magic, Town Life and Country Life, Children, Kings,* and there are many more.

READING THE PLAYS

Reading Shakespeare three-dimensionally is at first quite a laborious business. Try skimming through the play (even if you know it well) without looking things up. If you tend to be forgetful, make a note of your first impressions; for the moment you are the audience, and a first impression is what they will have. A general idea of what happens will form in your mind, the salient characters, the most interesting events, the most lucid bits of writing. If the play attracts you, thousands of inventive ideas will surge into your head and probably you will begin to trace a coherent thread, a pattern of action. If they don't and you can't, look at another play. There is no point in doing a play that doesn't excite you.

2 Preparing the Text

GENERAL THOUGHTS

Think of the text as if it were in a foreign language. This may seem unduly pessimistic or even frivolous. But open the Collected Works at random; you won't find many lines without an unfamiliar word or construction. Take this passage:

> O world! thy slippery turns. Friends now fast sworn,
> Whose double bosoms seem to wear one heart,
> Whose hours, whose bed, whose meal, and exercise,
> Are still together, who twin, as 'twere, in love
> Unseparable, shall within this hour,
> On a dissension of a doit, break out
> To bitterest enmity...
>
> (*Cor* 4.4.12)

The gist is clear, but do you know *exactly* what it means, without notes, or glossary or time to think? Without precise understanding your acting will be woolly. Shakespeare's vocabulary, grammar and syntax all need to be studied if you are to be a fluent Shakespearian.

The verse imposes other problems. It is not natural to speak in iambic pentameters, nor are they very easy to listen to, even if you're poetically inclined. Shakespeare's verse needs the right accent, like French or Xhosa. You must bluff your audience into believing that you're chatting away in good Shakespeare-ese. You will need to cultivate a good ear, a feeling for intonation and rhythm, and for the weight and length of syllables, and you must be able to place your speech in the right part of your mouth, like any good linguist (see Chapter 5). Learning a language takes time and patience, but don't be daunted. Shakespeare is so rarely abstruse that the cruces are usually blamed on textual corruption. As long as *you* are absolutely clear about what you are doing and feeling, your audience will follow you and enjoy you even if they only understand some of what you're saying: Shakespeare will see to that. However, you won't give a lucid performance until you understand the text, and for that you will need some editorial help. So that the first requisite of a good Shakespeare production is:

A Good Text

The right texts for actors are not necessarily the most scholarly ones with the most notes, in fact the less formidable a script looks and feels the better. Avoid the big Collected Works, for instance, with the columns of tiny print. *Signet Classics* paperback editions (General Editor: S Burnet, NEL) are often used by professional companies; they are readably printed with brief notes and paraphrases at the foot of each page (to obviate fumbling about), a good introduction, an account of sources and helpful selected criticism. They are not expensive and cover all the plays, as does the *New Penguin* edition (edited by T J B Spencer and S Wells). Each play has an introduction and notes on the text, but the commentary and glossary is inconveniently (from the actor's viewpoint) at the back of the text.

There should be at least one *Arden* edition to hand during rehearsals to help with textual problems (edited by H F Brooks and H Jenkins, published by Methuen). Most plays are currently available in *Arden* paperbacks. This edition is intended for advanced students, and the notes and comments (at the foot of each page of text) are scholarly and detailed. There is a long critical introduction, and relevant extracts from the sources.

The *New Cambridge Shakespeare* (General Editor: J D Wilson, CUP) is a more venerable edition for students, and is also in paperback. It is less useful to actors because the notes and separate glossary are at the back and the print is intimidating.

Schools editions are often attractive and excellent for performers, particularly when they have notes and paraphrases on the opposite page to the text. A selection:

The *New Warwick Shakespeare* (General Editor: S Gardner, Blackie) has a short introduction, and the following titles are available to date: *Ham, Lear, Mids N, Temp, 1 Hen IV, Macb, Twel N, Jul C, Merch V, Oth.*

The Players' Shakespeare, (Editor: J H Walter, Heinemann). Some of the notes are put in question form. There are articles on Elizabethan theatre, dating, sources and points of interest. Titles: *Twel N, Merch V, Rom & Jul, Ant & Cl, Ham, Oth.*

The Macmillan Shakespeare (Macmillan Educational) has articles on sources, background and good explanatory notes opposite. Titles: *Twel N, Temp, Macb, Ham, Jul C, Rom & Jul, AYL, Rich III, Tam Shr, Merch V, Lear, Rich II, 1 Hen IV*.

The New Swan Shakespeare (General Editor: B Lott, Longman) is slanted towards students of English as a second language; the thorough explanation of words is often illuminating, and there are drawings, paraphrases and notes opposite the text.

All schools editions mentioned are in paperback as well as hard covers.

ACTING EDITIONS

The only acting editions of Shakespeare are those of George Skillan (published by Samuel French). The plays are presented in a neat, pre-directed package, with introduction, basic staging, designs, cuts, glossary and a directorial running commentary. Some of the staging is old-fashioned, but the directional advice is usually searching and sensitive. You will find these editions very useful if you are baffled by a difficult scene, and the commentaries are recommended reading for student-actors.

Editions of the following are available: *Ant & Cl, AYL, Ham, Hen V, Hen VIII, Jul C, Lear, Macb, Merch V, Merry W, Mids N, Oth, Rich II, Rich III, Rom & Jul, Tam Shr, Temp, Twel N*.

THE FIRST FOLIO

It is important at least to have a look at your play in the Folio, and/or in Quarto if one exists. The Folio is not, as some people imagine, an indecipherable tome of Elizabethan scrawl. It is easy to read and wonderfully vivid and exciting to handle, and you cannot fail to be moved by the thought that these are the texts prepared and read by Shakespeare's friends and contemporaries. A more practical reason for consulting the Folio is that it yields performance clues, in the punctuation particularly, which later editions have carefully tidied out of existence (see pp. 31f, 57f and below for more on this subject).

The best facsimile Folio is the *Norton*, prepared by Charlton Hinman and published by Hamlyn (1968). In the OUP edition prepared by H Kökeritz (1955) the print is reduced to one-fifth.

1. PREPARATION

Armed with a comfortable text, the performer now opens battle with the words. If you are methodical at this stage you will help yourself tremendously towards a vivid performance and also to painless line-learning. Here is a suggested plan of campaign for each actor (the director must of course prepare the whole play in this kind of way):
(a) Clip a piece of paper to the back inside cover of your script. Write on it:
  (i) A personal glossary of unfamiliar words in your part, such as coinages or archaisms, and
  (ii) A list of words that sound familiar but mean something else. Some common ones that often cause confusion are:

accomplish (to equip)	honest (chaste)
affect (to aim at, or love)	huddle (pile up)
apt (ready, willing)	idle (foolish)
avoid (to get rid of, or to depart)	jump (to agree, or to risk)
brave (fine, excellent)	naughty (worthless)
capable (impressionable)	nice (fastidious, or trivial or
conceit (imagining)	accurate)
curious (anxious, or delicate)	peevish (silly)
determine (to end)	period (conclusion)
favour (face)	practice (trick)
get (beget)	sensible (capable of feeling)
	shrewd (malicious)

C T Onion's *A Shakespeare Glossary* (OUP, 1911 revised 1953) is a useful book to have around during rehearsals.
(b) Look up classical allusions in the notes or in an encyclopedia or in Brewer's *Dictionary of Phrase and Fable*. Allusions are seldom merely for decoration; look for their reverberations. Take this example from *Twelfth Night*. Viola is waiting to see Olivia and has been intercepted by Feste, whom she tips a coin:

Feste Would not a pair of these have bred, sir?
Viola Yes, being kept together and put to use.
Feste I would play Lord Pandarus of Phrygia, sir, to bring a Cressida to this Troilus.
Viola I understand you, sir; 'tis well begged. (*Tips him again*)
(3.1.56)

The Pandarus reference is funny because everyone knows that Pandarus was a go-between for Troilus and Cressida; but the clown also means that if Viola tips him again he will bring Olivia (as it were Cressida) to her (as it were Troilus). This thought is in keeping with Feste's unromantic nature; it might give a salacious, Pandar-like colouring to his voice, and he could illustrate bringing an imaginary coin to the one already in his hand. To complicate matters, Viola herself is a go-between for Orsino (as it were Troilus) and Olivia, and remembering this, her 'I understand you, sir' might well be self-conscious. To both Feste and Viola and to most of the audience Troilus and Cressida are a symbol of unprosperous love, which is ironically appropriate at this moment. All these tiny details may seem academic, but they are worth thinking about; anything that helps you to become part of Shakespeare's imaginative world will also enrich your acting. (See p. 41 for more on classical references.)

(c) Here are two methods of unravelling a text which might be more interesting than straightforward paraphrasing:

   (i) For the moment ignore the verse lines and think of your text as prose. Isolate each sentence and read it aloud, making sure that you understand the syntax as well as the vocabulary. Now imagine that a confidant is asking you a series of questions or making remarks, to which the lines of your script are the answers. For example, Viola's soliloquy at *Twel N* 2.2.18:

Statement That man says you left a ring with Olivia.
Answer *I left no ring with her.*
Statement He says that she says you did.
Answer *What means this lady?*
Question Could it mean that she has fallen for your handsome exterior?
Answer *Fortune forbid my outside have not charmed her.*
Question Can you remember how she looked at you?
Answer *She made good view of me . . .*

Even if the text is complicated and highly figured, try to find the simplest possible prompting statement.

   (ii) Ask a fellow actor to imagine that they have never heard a word of Shakespeare. Address your text to them slowly; they should stop you and ask you to explain everything they don't understand. Or you could pretend you were

Shakespeare reading a first draft of his play to the director of the National Theatre.

(d) Listen in rehearsal to other people's lines and make sure you understand *them*, especially if you have to answer or address them. If you don't understand them, tell them so.

Until you know exactly what the words mean, you can't start the exciting business of acting. Dedicated actors don't need encouragement to work on their own, but it may be more practical for a school group to go through the text as an ensemble; much depends on their scope and maturity, and the director must decide on the best approach. The important thing is for everyone to be fresh, interested and confident. Rehearsals musn't become submerged in boring academic discussions; if you must discuss, be as brief as you can. Straight read-throughs of the play in first rehearsals are usually a depressing waste of time.

Remember that Shakespeare is vast. It takes time to adjust the ear to the sound of the verse and the archaic English, and lifetimes to pick up all the resonances of a text. You will find it best to take things gradually, dealing with difficult passages as you rehearse each scene.

2. Editing

'The blue pencil is a dangerous weapon,' wrote the sensible Shakespearian Harley Granville-Barker. '. . . It solves too many little difficulties far too easily.' Votaries of the Bard do not like cutting his text, in fact the tiniest transposition of words will cause them personal anguish. However, you may have a young cast, a suspicious audience, too few actors or not enough rehearsal time. You may simply want to keep the play short; whatever the *Romeo and Juliet* Prologue says, without cutting, most of the plays run almost three hours. Clearly, they were trimmed for performance at the Globe. How you cut depends on your personal sense of reverence, but here are some general guidelines:

(a) It's justifiable to cut utterly arcane or topical allusions, of which there are few.

(b) Whether or not you cut obscenities depends on the ability of the actors to cope with them. The chances are they will either be impenetrably Elizabethan or thoroughly enjoyed.

(c) It is better to trim long dull scenes than to risk losing your audience's attention. For example, the Four Gentlemen scene in *Wint T* (5.2), the second and fourth scenes of *Henry V* and the first Greek scene of *Tr & Cr* (1.3) are notorious slumber-traps (although they only need imaginative acting). But make sure that your cuts don't create obscurities instead of removing them.

(d) You will want to trim funny bits if the actors can't enliven them, particularly the duels of wit in the early plays. Badinage like this badly performed is likely to send a village-hall audience into a trance of boredom:

Mercutio Nay, I am the very pink of courtesy.
Romeo Pink for flower.
Mercutio Right.
Romeo Why, then is my pump well flowered.
Mercutio Well said: follow me this jest now till thou hast worn out thy pump, that, when the single sole of it is worn, the jest may remain after the wearing sole singular.
Romeo O single-soled jest! solely singular for the singleness!, etc etc.
(*Rom & Jul* 2.4)

Try to snip here and there rather than leave out scenes or huge chunks, or you will spoil Shakespeare's careful and necessary plan (and risk enraging the Bardophiles in your audience). Scenes like the Carriers (1 *Hen IV* 2.1), the Clown in *Othello* or the Musicians in *Romeo and Juliet* 4.4 are often omitted because they are difficult to make funny or seem irrelevant; but they are there for vital tension-relaxing and atmosphere-building purposes. In general nothing is superfluous or overweighted, and injudicious chopping creates horrible holes. To quote Granville-Barker again: 'We cut and carve the body of a play to its peril.' All this will become clearer during the course of rehearsals.

As a general principle, look out for qualifying or exemplifying phrases which neither move the action on nor convey vital character information. Obviously it is brutish to mangle the metre or the meaning. Here is a speech of Lady Hotspur's with possible cuts and justifications:

> O, my good lord! why are you thus alone?
> For what offence have I this fortnight been
> A banished woman from my Harry's bed?
> Tell me, sweet lord, what is't that takes from thee
> Thy stomach, pleasure, and thy golden sleep?

[*Why dost thou bend thine eyes upon the earth,*
And start so often when thou sitt'st alone?
Why hast thou lost the fresh blood in thy cheeks,
And given my treasures and my rights of thee
To thick-eyed musing and curst melancholy?]

> These lines do not add to the audience's information; and there is another immediate description lower. 'Sleep' connects with 'slumbers'.

In thy faint slumbers I by thee have watched,
And heard thee murmur tales of iron wars,
[*Speak terms of manage to thy bounding steed,*]

> Could go. Difficult line for modern audience and 'bounding steed' is now almost comical.

Cry, 'Courage! to the field!' And thou hast talked
Of sallies and retires, of trenches, tents,
[*Of palisadoes, frontiers, parapets,*
Of basilisks, of cannon, culverin,]

> The effect of strange piled-up words is achieved without these lines.

Of prisoners' ransom, and of soldiers slain,
And all the currents of a heady fight.
Thy spirit within thee hath been so at war,
[*And thus hath so bestirred thee in thy sleep,*]

> Could go, because by now we know that she is describing H. asleep.

That beads of sweat have stood upon thy brow,
Like bubbles in a late-disturbed stream;
[*And in thy face strange motions have appeared*
Such as we see when men restrain their breath
On some great sudden hest. O! what portents are these?]

> After the keen bubble image these lines do not make an essential point, and rather suggest padding: the Bard not quite at his best. The exclamation is difficult for the actress.

Some heavy business hath my lord in hand,
And I must know it, else he loves me not.

(*1 Hen IV* 2.3.42)

3. ADAPTING

If you're planning a musical version of *Macbeth*, or if you propose to rewrite your text in modern English, or to embody it in a play of your own (à la *Rosencrantz and Guildenstern Are Dead*) or to introduce contemporary relevance (*The Shrew*), then you are not, of course, performing Shakespeare and you won't be needing this book.

If you are considering a very much reduced version of the original you will find some useful comments in the introduction to *The Wars of the Roses* by Peter Hall and John Barton (BBC 1970). The authors point out in defence of their version that (a) any stage production is in a sense an adaptation, in that it is a selection by the performers of all the possible ways of doing the play, and (b) if you're going to adapt, it is less heinous to hew texts of which Shakespeare's authorship is doubtful, or which are not very familiar. The *Wars of the Roses* itself is a good example of how to revamp a text and fill in gaps with convincing pseudo-Shakespearian verse.

Rewriting corrupt or peculiar bits is allowed. The first act of *Titus Andronicus*, for example, does not make much sense as it stands. You may feel that you should change obscure words, but this is dangerous practice; where do you stop? Take the word 'scour' in

> Behind the tuft of pines I met them; never
> Saw I men scour so on their way
>
> (*Wint T* 2.1.34)

The current meaning of the word makes the line positively comic. You could substitute 'hurry' or 'so hurry' or 'speed', but you lose the particular weight of Shakespeare's diphthong, which is carefully placed in the line for the actor to stress precisely as Shakespeare wanted it to be stressed. It is a vivid and interesting word, and as long as the actor informs it with the right meaning (having meticulously perused the *OED*) the audience will understand and enjoy it.

4. BACKGROUND READING

You may well be bemused by the range of existing Shakespeariana. Which of the thousands of enticing books should you go for?

Should you read about the play before rehearsals? How much background reading is necessary to a good production? The best test of a book about Shakespeare is whether it stimulates you to powerful and enthusiastic invention. You will no doubt be bringing your own fresh point of view to the production. It is a pity to base a production on someone else's ideas. The danger of reading criticism at this stage is that you may lose confidence in your own ideas, or even forget them. Also, if time is short you don't want to be distracted from the play into abstract discussions, fascinating though they may be. For these reasons it may be best to limit your reading to social histories, biographies or contemporary documents, anything which helps you to identify with Shakespeare's intentions in his writing, and to enter the living world of the plays. However, if you're stuck with a difficult staging problem, or lose your first delight in a play, it can be refreshing to look at it from someone else's point of view, and critical works are no more than a compendium of these.

Shakespeare: A Study and Research Guide, by D M Bergeron (Macmillan, 1976) hacks a very helpful path through the jungle of Shakespeariana. You might also consult *Shakespeare: Select Bibliographical Guides*, S Wells (OUP, 1973) or the annual bibliography in the *Shakespeare Quarterly* (see p. 19).

BOOKS FOR INFORMATION

General and Biographical

Everyone should have a general idea of Shakespeare's life and the circumstances of the plays, and should know about the shape of an Elizabethan theatre. Such primary facts are provided in the prefatory remarks to the Signet edition; there is a good outline under Shakespeare in the New Columbia Encyclopedia, or, in more detail, there is G E Bentley's Shakespeare: *A Biographical Handbook* (Yale Univ Press, 1961). Of the biographies, *Shakespeare of London* by Marchette Chute (Dutton, 1949, and Souvenir, 1977) is excellent, *Shakespeare* by Anthony Burgess (Cape and Penguin, 1970) is racy, readable and well illustrated, and so is *Shakespeare: A Pictorial Biography* by F E Halliday (Thames & Hudson, 1956). All three of these authors evoke a realistic setting for their subject. Good, brief, general books which discuss the plays in sequence are *Introducing Shakespeare* by G B Harrison (Penguin, 1939) and *The Essential Shakespeare* by J D Wilson (CUP, 1932). Both the original and *The New Companion to Shakespeare Studies* (editors H Granville-Barker and G B Harrison (CUP, 1934) and by K Muir and S Schoenbaum (CUP, 1971) are solid introductions, and include essays on background, music, sources and criticism.

Everyman's Companion to Shakespeare, G and B Lloyd Evans (Dent, 1978) provides useful information, such as lists of characters, a glossary of hard words, synopses of plots and historical facts about Shakespeare productions.

Historical Setting

The company should know something about the social and political setting of the plays. The following will probably need to be explained, especially to a school cast:
(a) The treatment of people low in the social order such as beggars, madmen, mobs and servants.
(b) The divinity of kings: a crucial issue in the history plays and to some extent in *Macbeth, Lear* and *Julius Caesar*.
(c) The position of wives. It is difficult for a modern girl to identify with a Kate, a Desdemona, an Hermione or a Helena without understanding that wifely obedience was part of the social order. Cuckoldry is no longer as humorous and horrific as it was once.
(d) Filial obedience and kinship. Important in *Temp, AYL, Tam Shr, Rom & Jul, Macb, Ham, Lear, Oth*.

A simple way of explaining the Elizabethan social scene would be to quote and discuss the degree speech from *Tr & Cr* 1.3.78, or the bees (*Hen V* 1.2.183). A very readable but now rather old-fashioned account of the social order is *The Elizabethan World Picture* by E M W Tillyard (Chatto, 1943, and Penguin, 1963). Idiosyncratic, but thorough, are: *The Elizabethan Renaissance: The Life of the Society* (1971) and *The Elizabethan Renaissance: The Cultural Achievement* (1972) by A L Rowse. A smaller, well illustrated book by the same author is *Shakespeare the Elizabethan* (1977). All three are published by Macmillan. *Queen Elizabeth I* by J E Neale (Cape, 1934, and Penguin, 1973) is an excellent perennial.

Books for the Imagination

The actors' imaginations must be encouraged to soar and sparkle, but some casts will not take kindly to having books thrust at them. In this case it is a good idea for the director to throw out exciting chunks of information at appropriate moments in rehearsal, in order to draw the performers into the world of the plays and make them feel Shakespearian in a real and robust way. There is really no limit to the work that can be done in this direction. Analogues or contrasts with twentieth-century life can be enjoyable. For *As You Like It*, for example, you could conjure up the reality of Court life, and explore its likeness to modern show-business: the hanging around, the intrigue, the boredom, the scandal, the break-throughs, the surface glitter. The country, in contrast, would have been lush and unruly, with tangled forests, wild fields and heaths, more flowers, insects and birds than now, empty spaces, no tarmac or pylons, and so on. The sort of topics which might provoke imaginative discussions are:

(a) The shortness, uncertainty and disease-riddenness of life. The plague is always a source of fascination. See F P Wilson: *The Plague in Shakespeare's London* (OUP, 1927).

(b) The fewness of people (the population of London in 1600 was about 200,000). People were rarer and therefore more interesting to each other; everyone knew about everyone else's affairs.

(c) The immediacy of the seasons, and the closeness of weather and countryside even to Londoners.

(d) London. Its geography and the importance of the river and its craft. You could track Shakespeare's lodgings and his movements. Stowe's *Survey of London* (Everyman, 1912) has some vivid information.

(e) The fewness of material possessions. Books, jewels and materials were precious commodities.

(f) Everyday behaviour. How it would have been affected by clothes (see Chapter 8). Extrovertism. Diet and drinking.

(g) Cruelty as exemplified by bear-baiting and public punishments. By modern standards social conscience was in its infancy.

(h) Communicating. To get on in the professions you had to be a good rhetorician. Many people were illiterate and therefore good at listening. News was communicated by spoken word, or broadside, or in ballads.

Some books which might inspire Elizabethan fantasies:

The Description of England (John Harrison) was first printed in 1577, and is invaluable for bringing Elizabethan England sharply to the imagination and senses; see especially 'On the Food and Diet of the English,' 'Of their Apparel and Attire', 'Of Gardens and Orchards' and 'Of our English Dogs and Their Qualities'. The most recent edition is by Georges Edelen (Cornell Univ Press, 1968). There is also a short Everyman edition.

Elizabethan and Jacobean Journals, compiled by G B Harrison (Routledge, 1938). These are anthologies of information from contemporary sources, arranged in chronological sequence for the years 1591–1609. They read like a daily newspaper, with the latest weather, plays, books, gossip, politics and current excitements.

Life in Shakespeare's England, compiled by J D Wilson (CUP and Penguin, 1949). A fine anthology of Elizabethan prose, covering all aspects of town and country life.

See also:

Alfred Harbage, *Shakespeare's Audience* (Columbia Univ Press, 1941). A scholarly, fascinating book.

St Clare Bryne, M, *Elizabethan Life in Town and Country* (Methuen, 1954)

Burton, Elizabeth, *The Elizabethans at Home* (illustrated, Secker & Warburg, 1958)

Ivor Brown, *How Shakespeare Spent the Day* (Bodley Head, 1963). All Ivor Brown's books are vivid and easy to read.

Martin Holmes, *Shakespeare and His Players* (Murray, 1972)

T R Henn, *The Living Image* (Methuen, 1972), deals with sport, hunting and war.

Novels

Novels are a not-to-be-despised means of historical spoon-feeding. For adults:

C Oman, *The Best of His Family* (Hodder & Stoughton, 1933)

J Brophy, *Gentleman of Stratford* (Harper NY, 1939)

A Burgess, *Nothing Like the Sun* (Heinemann, 1964)

J Mortimer, *Will Shakespeare* (Delacorte, 1977). The book of the television series.

And for children:

M Dallow, *The Heir of Charlecote* (Cassell, 1938)

M Jowett, *A Cry of Players* (OUP, 1961)
M Chute, *The Wonderful Winter* (Dent, 1962)

Criticism

The small OUP collection, *Shakespearian Criticism*, edited by D Nichol Smith (1930), is a useful anthology of pre-twentieth-century criticism. Coleridge, Hazlitt and Lamb are always thought-provoking, Coleridge especially. See *Coleridge's Shakespearian Criticism* (2 vols) edited by T M Raysor (Constable, 1930).

Some stimulating recent works:

J R Brown, *Shakespeare and his Comedies* (Methuen, 1957)
E F K Ludowyk, *Understanding Shakespeare* (CUP, 1962)
D Traversi, *Shakespeare: The Roman Plays* (Stanford Univ Press, 1963)
Shakespeare: The Tragedies essays edited by A. Harbage (Prentice-Hall, 1964)
M Davies, *Shakespeare for the Sixth* (Univ Tutorial Press, 1969). A simple general introduction.

Stagecraft Books

The most important, and quite small, category of books for your purpose is the one dealing with Shakespearian stage conditions, and how to imagine, enjoy and recreate them. Harley Granville-Barker's *Prefaces to Shakespeare* (Sidgwick & Jackson) are essential reading for performers. Fourteen plays are treated in detail, and the general approach uniquely illuminates the whole question of staging and interpretation. They are available in paperback (Batsford) in 6 volumes: (1) *Hamlet*, (2) *Lear, Ant & Cl*, (3) *Jul C, Cymb, Merch V*, (4) *Oth, LLL*, (5) *Rom & Jul, Cor*, (6) *Wint T, Twel N, Mids N, Macb*.

See also:

R Watkins, *On Producing Shakespeare* (Michael Joseph, 1950). A most inspiring book to which this text is much indebted.
A M Nagler, *Shakespeare's Stage* (Yale, 1958). Concise and interesting.
L Hotson, *Shakespeare's Wooden O* (Hart-Davis, 1958)
B Beckermann, *Shakespeare at the Globe* (Macmillan NY, 1962)
I Smith, *Shakespeare's Globe Playhouse* (Scribner's, 1963)
G E Bentley, *Shakespeare and his Theatre* (Univ of Nebraska, 1964)
J L Styan, *Shakespeare's Stagecraft* (CUP, 1967)
C W Hodges, *The Globe Restored*, and for children *Shakespeare's Theatre* (OUP, 1968)
A Gurr, *The Shakespearean Stage* (CUP, 1970)

Each author interprets the few known facts in his own way, but any one of these books will give you a graphic idea of a Globe performance.

Journals

You might enjoy reading articles in Shakespearian journals. They have the advantage of being short and up-to-the-minute and they cover all possible topics. Consult the index of whichever journal is easily obtainable through your local library. The *Shakespeare Survey* (Cambridge) is particularly useful because of its annual reviews of works on Shakespeare. The American *Shakespeare Quarterly* (Folger Shakespeare Library) includes reviews of productions of the year in the US and England, and an annual bibliography.

Finally, the director and cast may know all there is to know about their play, but what about the audience? Should they be supplied with a dossier of programme notes? It seems an imposition. All you can really do about the state of your audience's background knowledge is to make your production clear and self-explanatory; or, at least, to make it so vital and refreshing that the audience will rush away to read all about it, or better still to read the play itself with new excitement.

3 Staging Shakespeare

Staging is a term which is sometimes applied to the whole business of putting a play on the stage, but is also used in a limited sense to mean the plotting of actors' moves and entrances (also known as *blocking*) and the working-out of difficult stage effects such as the 'queynt devise' in *The Tempest*, processions, fights, dances and so on. Staging is the director's overall responsibility because he/she is best situated to see the stage and the shape the actors make upon it. Like the editor of a newspaper, the director initiates policies, puts the team to work and finally decides what to present to the public. He/she should be an inspiring leader and a tactful coordinator, and must seethe with energy.

The first part of this chapter discusses how a knowledge of Shakespeare's stage can help you with your production. The second part describes a way of exploring the text for directorial clues.

THE HISTORICAL APPROACH

You will have chosen your play for a specific reason: either because it is a set text for GCE, or because you have the right actor for the lead or—with luck—because you love it. Many ideas for its staging, in the wider sense, will have occurred to you. You may have an overall conception: *As You Like It* costumed in green boiler suits, for instance; a *Julius Caesar* set in fascist Italy, *Cymbeline* on ice. You may have worked out the whole production in miniature with matchsticks. Or you may be thumbing nervously through your text wondering what on earth to 'do' with it.

It is worth sitting down for a moment to consider the situation coolly. You are handling a script written about 350 years ago wh ch contains minimal explicit instruction for stage presentation. It was written to be performed on a particular stage, or stages, by actors well known to the author, in order to please a particular audience. In its time the play was probably a wild success; its author, at any rate, made his fortune.

In some respects, it may be remote from the everyday experience of your own audience. You will want to make them aware of the play's excellencies, and at the same time to entertain them. You want them to have a good evening, not a boring one. You know that the play in your hands is one of the best ever written. As far as your production is concerned, this is its first performance for about 350 years. Try to scrape away any literary accretions, or memories of traditional staging or performances you may have seen. Start from scratch.

Less than 100 years ago, Shakespeare was performed rather as grand opera is performed today, with elaborate, true-to-life sets, and dozens of extras. Famous soliloquies were delivered like arias, sometimes to applause; rude bits were expunged. There were even intervals between the acts. No-one any longer imagines that Shakespeare should be performed operatically; views of Verona, sphinxes, Scottish castles with martlets' nests and suchlike are no longer requisite, and picture-frame stages are fast becoming a part of history. In this century, the plays make best sense when they are performed as Shakespeare wrote them to be performed, and the chief credit for this astonishingly simple discovery is due to William Poel, who experimented with neo-Elizabethan productions at the turn of the century, and to Harley Granville-Barker, who put many of Poel's principles into practice in his professional productions at the Savoy in the 1920s. Granville-Barker laid down what are still essential guidelines for performers in his *Prefaces*. (For the fascinating history of Shakespeare production Robert Speaight's *Shakespeare on the Stage* (Collins, 1973) is recommended.)

So your first step is to find out about staging in Shakespeare's theatres *c* 1600. Amazingly little is actually known. Most of the books on the subject are full of brilliant guesswork. Your own theories, based solidly on the evidence, are as good as anybody's.

The following is a summary of the available evidence. (Those to whom it is familiar should skip to p. 29.)

1. Stages

Shakespeare's plays were performed in the Globe playhouse, in a hall in Blackfriars and in other halls and houses in London and the country. There were two Globes on the same south bank site: the first was burned down in 1613 and the second, more sumptuous, was pulled down in 1644. They were either round or polygonal. Maps and engravings from the late sixteenth and early seventeenth centuries show various shapes. Shakespeare describes what was probably the Globe as a 'cockpit' and a 'wooden O' in the first *Hen V* Chorus.

The only graphic evidence of the inside of an Elizabethan playhouse is A van Buchel's copy of a drawing by a Dutch visitor (*c* 1596), known as the de Witt drawing. This shows the Swan theatre, which also stood on the south bank. For an indifferent sketch, it is certainly the most pored-over in the world. It is reproduced in many books on Shakespeare, among them: *The Elizabethan Stage*, volume II by Chambers, *The Globe Restored* by C W Hodges, and *Shakespeare on the Stage* by Speaight. The enormous stage, looking misleadingly like a piece of plywood, projects halfway across a circular area, and is half covered by a canopy supported on ornate pillars, painted, according to de Witt, to look like marble. The forestage is supported on two wispily drawn shapes which might be anything. There are two doors set in the upstage back wall. Three actors, well downstage, are performing what looks like (but isn't) *Twelfth Night*. A row of unidentifiable people are sitting in a backstage gallery. The orchestra indicated to the right of the stage was a sort of box for important people, as in the Roman theatre.

In 1664 in his *Discourse of the Stage*, Richard Flecknoe described the earlier Elizabethan stages as 'but plain and simple, with no Scenes, nor Decorations of the Stage, but only old Tapestry, and the Stage strewed with rushes with habits (clothes) accordingly.' However, this was written twenty years after the second Globe was pulled down.

Building contracts for two theatres, the Fortune and the Hope, have survived. The stage at the Fortune was 43 feet wide and reached halfway across the 55-foot-square yard. In other respects it was based on the Globe. There were three tiers, or galleries, of seats and the building was open to the sky. All that is known of the Blackfriars hall, which the Globe company used from about 1496 until well after Shakespeare's death, is that it was 66 feet by 46 feet and had a stage, seating and galleries.

Behind the stage was the tiring house, or dressing rooms. How many rooms, and how you got to them, is not clear.

2. Scenery and Props

There is more documentary evidence about the staging of the plays than about the shape of the theatres, but the two sorts of evidence do not exactly illuminate one another. There is nothing to tell us how an Elizabethan actor walked on to a stage, how he looked and sounded, and what the stage looked like. The evidence that there is makes up a tantalizing scrapbook. But in a city surging with inventive theatre people and enthusiastic audiences, with at least fifteen playhouses, each with a different play daily, staging and acting styles were likely to have been diverse and developing. During Shakespeare's lifetime, as companies grew more prosperous and audiences more sophisticated, stage machinery and illusions became more elaborate and cunning. This is reflected in the changing type of stage effect in Shakespeare's plays; the technical demands of the early *Henry VI*s are quite different from those of the late *Tempest*.

Here is some evidence which is relevant to performers:

(a) The Henslowe Papers (edited Foakes and Rickert, 1961). These are notebooks and accounts kept by the manager of the Rose, Philip Henslowe, between 1589 and 1591. They list interesting props and costumes. For example:

Item, viii lances, i payer of stayers for Fayeton
Item, ii stepells, & a chyme of belles, & i beacon.
Item, i wooden canepie; owld Mahemetes head.
Item, ii moss banckes, & i snake.
Item, i poopes miter.
Bowght a robe for to goo invisibell . . .

These items gleam somewhat opaquely in the imagination. 'A robe for to goo invisibell.' What did it look like? A sort of black, hooded arrangement, like a manipulator's in the Bunraku theatre? Might that not look like a monk? Or was it white and diaphanous like a wisp of smoke? What were the moss banks made of? How were the pieces of scenery moved, and where stored?

(b) The English Wagner Book of 1590 (quoted by Chambers, *Elizabethan Stage* II.71). Faustus's servant Wagner weaves an astonishing vision of a transcendental playhouse:

> They might distinctly perceive a goodly Stage to be reared (shining to sight like the bright burnished golde) upon many a fair pillar of clearest Crystal, whose feet rested upon the Arch of the broad Raynebow, therein was the high Throne wherein the King should

sit, and that proudly placed with two and twenty degrees to the top, and round about curiously wrought chairs for diverse other Potentates, there might you see the ground work at the one end of the stage whereout the personated divels should enter in their fiery ornaments, made like the broad wide mouth of an huge Dragon... the teeth of this hell mouth far out-stretching. At the other end in opposition was seen the place where in the bloodles skirmishes are so often performed on the Stage, the Walls of iron... environed with high and stately Turrets of the like metal and beauty, and hereat many in-gates and out-gates; out of each side lay the bended Ordinances, showing at their wide hollows the cruelty of death; out of sundry loops many large banners and streamers were pendant, briefly nothing was there wanting that might make it a fair Castle. There might you see the Gibbet, the Posts the Ladders, the tiring house, there everything which in the like houses either use or necessity makes common. Now above all was there the gay clouds Usque Quaque adorned with the heavenly firmament, and often spotted with golden tears which men call stars...

Vision or no, this conveys quite a complex stage structure for martial plays like the *Henry VI*s.

(c) The plays themselves carry a few explicit directions. Some of these are fairly incorporeal. 'Enter above'. What exactly was this 'above'? It varies in function from castle walls to windows. The de Witt sketch shows a gallery stuck well back under the canopy; if there was a similar gallery at the Globe, it may have been used for spectators, or musicians, or for prologues or brief scenes. It is too narrow and remote for long scenes; the actors would have been cramped and the audience bored. At the Globe, possibly, there was a much wider gallery without the balustrade. We do not know.

It is highly likely that an 'above' was often constructed. Houses of scaffolding, covered with canvas or other material, were used in mediaeval pageants and mystery plays, and the Elizabethans probably built quite complex but mobile structures to represent houses, castles, walls, and cities. There is of course no balcony mentioned in the so-called balcony scene in *Rom & Jul*. The boy who played Juliet evidently did not feel or look diminished, as would a modern actress, by being only half in view at a window. But where the window was, whether in a permanent or a temporary structure, remains a mystery. 'Down, down I come,' says Richard II; he exits from 'above'; twenty-one words later, he has arrived 'below'. How? Visibly? Rushing down an inner staircase? This 'above' can't have been very high.

'Thus I enforce thy rotten jaws to open,' says Romeo to Juliet's tomb. There is room in this tomb for 4 prostrate and at least 10 upright people to participate in a scene of some 250 lines. What was this tomb, and where? Other well-chewed-over puzzles are the reference to the monument in *Ant & Cl* 4.13.8, 'passing over' the stage (how? where?) and 'enter at several doors' (how many and where were they?).

All that is really certain is that upper, lower or inner areas are indicated in nearly every play, and that the use of different levels in the theatre, as in a painting, is always interesting to the eye and useful to the dramatist.

3. Stage Dressing

Flecknoe's reference to old tapestry and rushes gives an impression of a stark, creaking sort of atmosphere at the Globe, and this has often been the style of twentieth-century productions, sometimes with Olde Tudor wattle-and-daub overtones. The idea of bareness has appealed to the current taste for austerity, and been supported by the ubiquitous need for economy. Brecht's staging methods were both influenced by and have influenced recent ideas about staging Shakespeare.

However, there is evidence to suggest that playhouse interiors were then quite gaudily decorated and there is evidence, too, that painted sets and backdrops were in use by Jacobean times. The playhouses probably varied in ornateness, depending on resources, but the Elizabethans loved colour, richness and illusion in their paintings; it would be odd if they liked the opposite in their playhouses.

4. Lighting and Effects

Performances took place in the afternoon, and presumably not when it rained (although there is a line in *Much Ado* which may have its origin in a comic ad lib: 'Stand thee close then under this penthouse for it drizzles rain . . .' 3.3.109). Torches, tapers, lanterns, etc, are often mentioned in the plays, and see also Henslowe's 'beacon'. There is no reason to suppose that these were not practical (and horribly hazardous); glimmering stage lights create excellent atmospherics and under the canopy and thatched galleries the stage was probably quite dim, especially on cloudy afternoons.

Thunder was made by rolling a cannon ball about, or with drums. Battle noises were provided by guns and fireworks; the latter may also have made lightning. It was a fired chamber during a performance of *Henry VIII* that set the first Globe on fire

And burnt downe both beame and snagg,
And did not spare the silken flagg.

(A 'Sonnett upon the pittiful burning of the Globe', quoted in Chambers II.421.)

A trapdoor was used, although not often by Shakespeare. In *Hamlet* it probably served both to remove the Ghost and as Ophelia's grave. Flying and descents were performed with the aid of machinery set up in the tiring house roof. Shakespeare does not often resort to these (see *Cymbeline* 5.4.93), although arguments have been advanced for flying witches in *Macbeth*, and Puck and Ariel on strings like bejerkined Peter Pans.

5. Costumes and Makeup

The main sources of evidence about costume are the Henslowe papers, a sketch by Henry Peacham of a performance supposedly of *Titus c* 1594, and the plays themselves.

Clearly, Shakespeare did not write his historical plays with historical costume as we know it in mind. *Julius Caesar* has references to doublets, cloaks, hats and nightcaps, Cleopatra tells Charmian to 'cut her lace' and the kitchen malkin in *Coriolanus* 2.2.227 pins on her best ruff before going to cheer her hero. History was not the scientific matter of thermoluminescence and potsherds that it is now, but a sort of semi-literary pursuit providing, as far as Shakespeare was concerned, a good source of plots. The Peacham sketch (whose authenticity is not fully established) shows a hotch-potch of styles rather like charades, and Titus certainly has a Roman-like tunic and a laurel wreath.

The costumes listed in the Henslowe papers are extremely expensive and sumptuous:

1 payer of whitte saten Venesons [venetians, or long breeches] cut with coper lace . . .
1 great pech coller dublet, with silver lace . . .
1 white and orange taney [tawny] skarf spangled . . .
1 black satten doublet, layd thyck with black and gowld lace.

There are also special items such as armour and 'i gostes sewt and i gosts bodeyes', and 'the clownes sewtes and hermetes sewtes with dievers other sewtes . . .'. All in all, the players wore fashionable and probably extravagant contemporary clothes (like actors in modern West End plays) which conveyed their status or profession instantly to the eye. Gangs were differentiated, to guide the audience: the blue versus the tawny coats of the Gloucester/Winchester factions in *Hen VI*, Greeks versus Trojans, Capulets versus Montagues, and so on.

Shakespeare's players would not have needed pancake in the daylit Globe, though the boys probably painted in imitation of whores and fine ladies. Animals' blood is known to have been used; Caesar would have a bladder of pig's blood under his doublet. Wounds, scars and diseases were somehow contrived; the bloody Coriolanus, the amputated Lavinia and perhaps the envenomed Ghost in Hamlet would have looked as terrifying as anything engendered in a twentieth-century film studio.

6. Speed

The 'two hours' traffic' of a play (see *Rom & Jul* Prologue I) is mentioned by many Elizabethan and Jacobean playwrights. Performances must have been very fast or very truncated. Countless vibrant, coherent modern productions have proved the effectiveness of speedy Shakespeare, although they have seldom been as short as two hours. Playing fast does not mean gabbling through the lines and galloping on and off stage. It means performing without long breaks for scene changes, and overlapping entrances and exits so that the scenes do not stop and start but melt interestingly into one another. It also means playing with a contained inner excitement that will generate the pace necessary to a good production.

7. Acting

Flecknoe in his *Short Discourse of the English Stage* (1664) says:

> It was the happiness of the Actors of those times to have such Poets as (these) to instruct them and write for them; and no less of those Poets to have such Docile and Excellent Actors to act their Playes.

During Shakespeare's lifetime the prestige of the common players rose high in England and indeed in the world, where it is still high today. But how they moved, stood, sounded in performance, what their particular stage quality was, is anyone's guess. From clues scattered through the plays (see e.g. Hamlet's speech to the Players, 3.2) and contemporary accounts, it seems that the mark of good acting was naturalism, a criterion that has not changed.

What physical effect did the new playhouses have on the players? In the de Witt sketch the acting area is well downstage and more or less in the geographical centre of the theatre. Thus no vital energy was squandered on projecting your voice and personality into the darkness of an unfathomable auditorium. Everything about the playhouses was an aid to effortlessness, reality, concentration and making powerful contact with your audience. The roundness and resonance of the Wooden O acted as a sort of visual and aural amplifier. You were, so to speak, in permanent close-up. You did not need to mouth or saw the air.

It is also important to remember that there has never been a time of such extraordinary creativity and excitement in the theatre. Shakespeare's plays are its culmination, but they are the progeny of the theatre world in which he worked, and this was peopled by strutting, competing, starry, admired actors, men who owned and organized their own theatre. There was no regiment of middlemen as there is today—executives, agents, directors, assistant directors, designers, etc—to exploit and harry them about. It is worth thinking about the sort of self-reliance and energy these actors might have exuded on stage.

8. Staging

Shakespeare evokes scenery with words.

How sweet the moonlight sleeps upon this bank! (*Merch V* 5.1.54)

But there were also props. A 'moss bancke' is one of the items listed by Henslowe. An Elizabethan theatre company was perfectly capable of producing furniture, and so no doubt is yours. Should you rely on the words alone to make their scenic effects, or do they need reinforcing with visual aids?

The question may seem impertinent. However, in any audience there is a range of imaginative response. Some people only believe in what they see, or in things that look real in the photographic sense; others react most powerfully to symbols. Probably the collective imagination of Shakespeare's audience was more creative than that of a modern audience, which is nourished on verisimilitude in films, photos and television, and certainly they were better listeners. But the Elizabethans were also delighted by realism (see *Merch V* 3.2.115-29) which is why they liked Holbein, Hilliard and good acting. If you think your audience collectively incapable of conjuring up moonshine, or if your Lorenzo's acting doesn't convey the moon and stars, by all means lay on a polystyrene bank, a follow spot, pattens of bright gold, and chirping crickets too, if you like. The words will weave their magic for those who can respond to them; the effects are there for those who can't.

Shakespeare's world was pleasantly uncluttered with objects by comparison with ours. His audience wouldn't have thought that a room furnished only by a chair and a stool was peculiarly bare, but today both actors and audience sometimes feel that a whole dimension of reality is missing. Actors feel naked without pockets to put hands in, cigarettes to smoke, windows to look out of. To audiences struggling to understand the text a bare stage may look bleak, especially if the acting is below par. And Shakespeare isn't easy to act. People nowadays are not used to communicating passion and imagination, to using their voices and bodies expressively on stage. The introduction of a few props and effects may be helpful to everyone.

Be guided by Shakespeare's own stage sense. He knew the dramatic power of a single, strong image, rather than lots of little distracting ones. Think of Yorick's skull or Desdemona's frail white handkerchief spotted with strawberries, produced at the perfect psychological moment.

In a recent production of *Twelfth Night* a taped sea sound was heard as a signature to the Orsino scenes, ('[My love] is all as hungry as the sea', 2.4.192), and also for Viola's first entrance and, most effectively, when she is reunited with Sebastian whom she had thought drowned. It was justified by the play's many sea references, and also because it was simple, emotional and undistracting.

To Summarize

The historical evidence provides you with important guidelines:
(a) *The Stage* If you can, make your stage or acting space a part of the audience, so that they are encouraged to concentrate.

Front row seats in a theatre are the most expensive because it is more enjoyable to watch from there than from anywhere else. Aim at providing each member of the audience with a front row seat. If you can vary the levels of your playing area, so much the better.

A small space, intelligently used, may be the best substitute for the arrangements of the Wooden O. A recent *Macbeth* was staged as a chamber piece, with the audience seated on three sides of a small acting area. The actors did not have to project unnaturally, with the result that their energy went into the play, which became charged with an extraordinary dense terror and power, like a neutron bomb. Most repertory theatres now have 'studios' (by analogy with film studios) where actors and audience can easily make contact. If you use a small space, be careful not to be misled by the proximity into giving a small or a lazy performance (see p. 46).

(b) *Scenery, Props and Effects* You actually need very little in the way of stage dressing, and the better your actors the less you will need. On the other hand, starkness and colourlessness are not compulsory, nor even desirable. Don't make the ghastly mistake of thinking that Shakespeare 'speaks for himself' in the theatre. He doesn't. He speaks through the minds and mouths of the people who act him. A cast standing around intoning the lines in jeans against black drapes is Starvation Shakespeare. Requisites are adaptable: you couldn't perform *Rom & Jul* 2.2 without an 'above', for instance; but it can be a balcony, a window or the top of a ladder hidden by a sheet or not hidden by a sheet, as your taste may incline. There are no rules about costumes, fights, lights, or any other aspect of Shakespearian staging.

(c) *The Acting* Whatever scenery you provide, it must allow for swift playing and clear narration. It must be an aid to the actors and not a substitute for them. You will find that Shakespeare is best illuminated by dynamic acting embodied in confident and delectable actors than by any amount of directorial superstructure (see Chapter 5 for ways of making actors delectable).

Directing Through the Text

When you come to decide how to move your actors around the stage, you will find that the text contains all the basic directions you need. If you have a facsimile First Folio now is the time to haul it out (see p. 7). If not, try to ignore all editorial addenda to the original stage directions. Many single editions put the additions in brackets.

Most instructions are obvious and logical. Take the first scene of *Twelfth Night*. Orsino enters with Curio and Lords. He is the centre of the scene, which is almost a monologue, so he must be positioned prominently. Music is playing either off stage or in a gallery (no entrance is indicated for Musicians in the Folio), so Orsino must raise his voice to speak to them. This identifies the setting as his own house. 'That strain again' makes the Musicians stop and sort themselves out for a reprise; Orsino carries on talking, until 'giving odour', where he pauses to listen; then he stops the music again with 'Enough, no more'. At 'Away before me' he waves the attendants off before exiting himself. All this is elementary.

There are more recondite clues. Notice the shape of the lines on the page. In the Folio they are all verse lines except for:

Cu. Will you go hunt my lord?
Du. What Curio?
Cu. The Hart.

There are three points to be made about these lines. Firstly, a change from verse to prose nearly always has a deliberate dramatic purpose. Here the prose interruption is abrupt, almost comic. Curio is being practical and hearty to jolt Orsino from his poetic moodiness. He mustn't pick up Orsino's tone, but cut across it. Secondly, most later editors have emended the lines thus, in order to make a pentameter of them:

Cu. Will you go hunt, my lord?
Or.   What, Curio?

If you accept this reading, you will agree that Curio and Orsino are sharing a line. This means that Orsino must chip in smoothly and be aware of the line as a whole. He can play his 'What, Curio?' with a start, as if interrupted in a reverie, or vaguely ('What did you say, Curio?'), or tragically ('What animal could I possibly want to hunt?'); but he must *complete* the line with his intention. Even if you don't like the emendation, notice that in the Folio divided lines usually indicate swift, overlapping thoughts and delivery. For example, the last 100 lines of *Lear* are distributed disjointedly to reflect the turmoil of the action. It is up to the director to make sure the text is paced and orchestrated as Shakespeare intended.

Thirdly, however you read the 'Hart' line, as a single foot of a pentameter (with the other 4 feet missing) or as a prose speech, its brevity is striking. What did Shakespeare mean by it? It leaves a gap, visibly on the page and dramatically in the action: in fact, it demands a pause, pregnant with Orsinesque brooding. Incomplete lines usually suggest a pause for action, not necessarily of a physical kind (see, for example *Othello* 4.3 lines 11, 79, 82, 90, 97, etc).

At line 24 the Folio reads:

   Or. Ere since pursue me. How now what newes from her?
                                                Enter Valentine

Editors, logically enough, have changed this to:

   Or. E'er since pursue me.
           Enter Valentine
   How now, what news from her?

The Folio compositor may simply have put the stage direction in the wrong place, or was trying to save a line. Or was he? The implication of the Folio layout is that Orsino calls out to the approaching Valentine either on or a split second *before* his entrance. This, plus the Lords' heads all turning, zooms the audience's attention sharply to Valentine (notice his name: he is not just A Messenger) and what he has to say, which is a vital piece of plot information. The emendation actually slows down this tiny piece of action, whereas in performance you need all possible punch and speed.

Imagery

Imagery is full of directorial clues. Notice its scope and violence here: death from surfeit, purging the air of pestilence, the hunted hart (Actaeon was torn to pieces by his own hounds), the arrow of love killing all Olivia's feelings except love, the surge and capacity of the sea. Notice too that Orsino has four 'O's to express his passion (see p. 42). All this is consistent with his romantic and hyperbolical character, and suggests a soaring, collapsing, agonizing mood. You must decide whether its sum effect is funny or serious.

Textual details like these are a good guide to the physical and psychological shape of a scene (the two aspects are interwoven, of course). They are mainly acting clues, and the director's function is that of a super-actor, who must explore every role in the play. This is why he needs plenty of time and energy.

Business

Inevitably, the clues will lead into ideas for business, comic or otherwise. This is as Shakespeare intended. If the actors want something to do they must have something. But keep it sensible. In a recent *Twelfth Night* the first scene began with Orsino, a sleek young man with a napkin tucked in his ruff, polishing off the carcass of a boar, and ended with him going off yawning for his siesta. Creative though the thinking was, it did not fit the implicit stage directions, and the tossing of bones and bustling of attendants became an irrelevant pantomime. The texts of *Coriolanus* and *Henry VIII* are unusually well stocked with genuine stage directions which show the kind of simple, real business that Shakespeare might have approved:

> Volumnia and Virgilia *set them down on two low stools and sew* (*Cor* 1.3)
> *The king is discovered sitting and reading pensively* (*Hen VIII* 2.2)
> *Exit King, frowning upon the Cardinal, the Nobles throng after him smiling and whispering.* (*Hen VIII* 3.2.)

One of the few bits of comic business recorded in the original text is in *1 Hen IV* 3.3. '*Enter the Prince and Poins marching. Falstaff meets them playing on his truncheon like a fife.*' Try to avoid clichés such as having Malvolio in outrageous night-gear, or irritating anachronisms such as having him turn around on 'Revolve' (*Twel N* 2.5.158), and don't invite laughs which destroy the intended orchestration of a scene.

There are 3 golden rules about business:
(a) Do less rather than more
(b) Only do it if you can do it well
(c) Don't be afraid to do none at all.

One of the hardest things to learn about performing Shakespeare is how to do nothing, to let your body rest; to act from stillness:

to trust to the action and passion of the words and let them support you (see next chapter).

A FINAL WORD ON STAGING

Though it is vitally important to root your production in the text, rehearsals should not turn into literary seminars. They should be creative, bubbling and experimental. A good Shakespeare production should be good show-business, as it was 350 years ago. It mustn't be restrained and over-reverent. It should crackle along, playing the laughs, the deaths, the ghosts, the effects, the sex and the sob-stuff blatantly. It must be joyful, even if it is a desperate play like *Timon* or *Troilus*. Don't be afraid of Shakespeare. One of the reasons for his survival is that he provides the best that the theatre can do, with more artistry, taste and truth than anyone else.

A NOTE TO THE DIRECTOR

You might find it interesting to keep a log book of the production, jotting down your own and the cast's ideas, good bits of inventiveness, and so on. If you are working well and creatively you will be amazed at the flow and change of thought between the beginning and end of rehearsals.

SOME BOOKS:

R Watkins, *Moonlight at the Globe. An Essay in Shakespeare Production* (Michael Joseph, 1946) and *On Producing Shakespeare* (Michael Joseph, 1950). Both contain inspiring practical advice.

C B Purdom, *Producing Shakespeare* (Pitman, 1950). A useful discussion of historical principles.

C de Banke, *Shakespearean Stage Production: Then and Now* (Hutchinson, 1954). The standard book on production from a practical viewpoint. Extensive bibliography, drawings of furniture, costumes, etc. Detailed descriptions of fabrics, music, dances, etc. Now a little dated.

J R Brown, *Free Shakespeare* (Heinemann Educational, 1974). The author suggests that there is too much directorial intervention in modern productions.

S Wells, *Royal Shakespeare*. Four Major Productions at Stratford-upon-

Avon (Manchester Univ Press, 1976). Shows how professional styles of production have changed since the 1950s.

Ralph Berry, *On Directing Shakespeare* (Croom Helm, 1977). Interesting interviews with professional directors, including Jonathan Miller and Trevor Nunn.

J C Trewin, *Going to Shakespeare* (Allen and Unwin, 1978). The author's experience of productions during the last 40 or so years.

Gareth and Barbara Lloyd Evans, *Everyman's Companion to Shakespeare* (Dent, 1978). A very useful book for directors. Includes a history of Shakespeare production, synopses of the plays and glossary.

R Flatter, *Shakespeare's Producing Hand* (Heinemann, 1948). A pioneer work on the directorial clues in the text.

4 Acting Shakespeare

CASTING

Casting is a matter of common sense. Remember that to act Shakespeare well you need intelligence and stamina. Physical shape can be changed on stage, but a stupid actor will not turn in a dynamic Hamlet. Encourage everyone to squeeze every drop of interest from their part, no matter how small. Contrary to belief, good small-part performers will not detract from main roles; on the contrary they are vital to a good production. Messengers, for example, shouldn't be mere walking placards, but responsible people who have travelled a long way with important news under their doublets. Everyone, star or supernumerary, should think of him/herself as a hero, and be discouraged from ironing her/himself out against the scenery.

Try to pick the best actors for the best parts. This is not as easy as it sounds. Your best Shakespearian actors will not necessarily be the loudest extroverts with the fruitiest voices. They will be warm, sexy and humorous, with healthy egos on the whole directed towards pleasing others. They will have vivid imaginations and enjoy working by themselves on the text and with others in rehearsal.

MAKING SHAKESPEARE REAL

Acting simply means pretending to be someone else and behaving as if you were that person in real life. A performance which is not real is always boring, no matter how famous or beautiful the actor is, or how sonorously he says his lines, and it is as boring in Shakespeare as it is in a modern play. On the other hand, real acting is enjoyable both for the actor and the spectator, and a person acting well becomes fascinating and attractive; this is an aspect of what is sometimes known as *theatrical magic*, and is always in short supply.

It is not easy to make Shakespeare real. Some performers bog themselves down in the language problems. There are even people who vaguely feel that because Shakespeare is 'poetic' or 'a classic' he should be acted in a rhetorical way with a good plummy delivery. Even the faintest whiff of this attitude produces a deathly performance. The problem remains: how can you sound real in iambic pentameters? Feel solid in nebulous or nonexistent surroundings? There are no authorial signposts of the 'sniffs', 'sits', 'stands', 'crosses DR', 'bridles', 'with a menacing laugh' variety, or neat packages of character information such as you might find in a Shaw play. All you are told is your name, or perhaps that you are King of France, Kinsman or Wife to Somebody, a Flattering Lord, or something obscure like Another Poet or a Gentle Austringer. You will have to start from scratch, writing your own directions and character information, basing yourself on a careful and imaginative scrutiny of the text.

Some Don'ts

Each time you read your lines (preferably aloud) something new will occur to you. Don't write down your directions to yourself, unless you are very absent-minded; you don't want to fix your ideas, but keep them in an exciting, creative, primeval-soup state. Don't read books at first to find out about your character, or the part will never live in your own brain and bloodstream. Read the play. You can read the books later. Pretend you are the first person ever to act the part. Don't think of it as an opportunity for self-aggrandizement. Be as concerned, as open-minded, as receptive as you can about the person you're playing.

The following guide to the character of Hotspur illustrates what sort of information to look out for in the text (*1 Hen IV*). Begin by establishing

(a) The Facts

Who is Hotspur? You will learn in the first scene that he is also called Harry Percy (1.1.53) and that he is the son of the Earl of Northumberland (1.1.80) and nephew of the Earl of Worcester (96). Later (1.3) you find out that he is married to Edmund Mortimer's sister. Also in the first scene you are told how Hotspur appears to others: he is young—decide how young—(53, 92 and 99), famous for his courage (81, 75, 42) and arrogant (92, 98–99).

Your primary information, therefore, is that you are a young, bellicose, conceited, Northern nobleman. Don't underestimate the importance of anchoring yourself on the solid facts, which Shakespeare provides punctiliously, both for your benefit and for the audience. It is astonishingly easy to forget that they are there. Think about what it means to be young, proud, warlike, brave and noble, not in a vague, general way, but as this *particular* person, Harry Percy. There is only one Hotspur, and only one Hotspur way of being proud and young.

(*b*) *Other People's Opinions*

Shakespeare often demonstrates that people are partly composed of what they are and partly of other people's reactions to them. You will learn a great deal from what other characters say about Hotspur. The King is envious, as a father, of his gallant reputation (1.1) but loses his temper when he comes face to face with him. Kate thinks he is capricious and neglectful of her (2.3) He is 'a mad-headed ape,' 'a giddy goose'. Falstaff calls him 'the mad fellow of the North' and 'gunpowder Percy'. To Northumberland he is 'a wasp-stung and impatient fool' (1.3.236). Hal admires him, sometimes ironically ('this gallant Hotspur, this all-praised knight' (3.2.140)), sometimes generously:

> ... this earth, that bears thee dead,
> Bears not alive so stout a gentleman.
>
> (5.4.92)

Worcester thinks that he is wilful and rude, 'a hare-brained Hotspur, governed by a spleen' (5.2.19), and summarizes severely:

> ... You are too wilful blame ...
> You must needs learn, lord, to amend this fault,
> Though sometimes it show greatness, courage, blood,
> Yet oftentimes it doth present harsh rage,
> Defect of manners, want of government,
> Pride, haughtiness, opinion and disdain ...
>
> (3.1.176)

All these opinions build up into the image of a large-spirited, energetic, undisciplined, rough sort of person, who is attractive and irritating at the same time. He must make the same complicated impression on the audience as he does on the other characters.

(c) *Details of Character*

Shakespeare's richest characters are stocked with interesting details which enormously help the actor to be real. The more details you can discover and weave vividly into your thought and feelings, the richer your characterization will be. Hotspur, for example, has passionate likes and dislikes. He doesn't like prim, mincing, affected people, or airy-fairy poetic people (1.3.36ff and 3.1.147 and 251). He hates poetry (3.1.130), and though he talks a great deal he doesn't think of himself as a good public speaker (5.2.91). Horses and fighting are what he likes best (2.3.94-107). He is brave (5.2.80-100 and 5.4.59-86), and doesn't mind smells, or pains and spartan living (1.3). He is not afraid of death. He is rude to people, including his wife, which means that he doesn't care about their feelings. Think about all these details: what sort of physical approach to life do they suggest?

(d) *First Appearance*

Shakespeare knew that people are tremendously influenced by first impressions, and he calculates carefully the effect of important characters' first appearances. Hotspur's first speech (1.3) is a superb gift to an actor; it conveys almost everything about Hotspur, and at the same time makes him appear attractive and witty. Never oidle on for your first entrance.

(e) *Humour*

Many of Shakespeare's attractive characters are funny, each in their special way. Think of Hamlet, Hal, Richard II, Richard III, Mercutio, Iago, Benedick, Beatrice, Rosalind, Viola. They do not raise guffaws, like the fools and clowns, but quiet grins. Very often in life people are attractive because they are funny, and vice versa. Don't try and puzzle out ways of being funny (unless slapstick is called for), but open yourself up to the humorous possibilities. Take Hotspur. Shakespeare gives the actor plenty of opportunity for mimicry, a schoolboyish, sending-up, showing-off form of humour which makes perfect sense in Hotspur. He could mimic the certain lord (1.3) or the King (1.3.159), the starling (1.3.225), the lack-brain of the letter (2.3), the kitten (3.1.118), Glendower (3.1.147 and 229), the comfit-maker's wife (3.1.251) and so on. He has comic habits such as talking too much (1.3) and being absent-minded (3.1.6 and 1.3.242). He also has some jokes which are in the rather small category of those that are amusing to modern audiences:

Lady P What is it carries you away?
Hotspur Why, my horse, my love, my horse.

(1.3.80)

(f) Detective Work

Once you are on the trail of your character, begin to scour the text for more subtle clues. Don't let this part of your preparation become academic or detached or over-analytical. Always try to respond with your senses and imagination. Think how freshly a child's imagination works, and how spontaneously children act/pretend. The Players in Hamlet have a child-like quality, as do many good actors today. Remember that Shakespeare wrote for actors, not for students of literature.

Use the *images and similes*. They are so to speak the spaces in the fabric of the play through which you can see into Hotspur's imaginative world. It is your prerogative as an actor to exploit them. For instance:

> I had rather be a kitten, and cry mew
> Than one of these same metre ballad-mongers;
> I had rather hear a brazen canstick turned,
> Or a dry wheel grate on the axle tree,
> And that would set my teeth nothing on edge,
> Nothing so much as mincing poetry;
> 'Tis like the forced gait of a shuffling nag.

(3.1.128)

The notes will tell you that copper candlesticks turned on a lathe make an odious noise. With a little effort you can evoke the screeching wheels of a cart, and you can imagine what riding a non-accelerating horse must be like to Hotspur. As you say the speech try and feel these images physically.

Here is a simple exercise. For each of the five senses jot down as many examples as you can of words or images used by your character. Thus, for Hotspur, under *hearing* you might put the canstick, the dry wheel, the lofty instruments of war, 'my lady the brach' howling, and the starling piping 'Mortimer'. Under *smell* you could have the sweetly perfumed lord, the slovenly corpse, the garlic and cheese in the windmill, the smoky house, the pepper gingerbread. For *touch*: being dry with rage and extreme toil, the new-shaven chin of the lord, being nettled and stung, the smarting wounds, the earthy and cold hand of Death upon his tongue, and so on.

Notice too how he uses images of women and weak milky things, to convey his own toughness: the lord is 'perfumed like a milliner', talks like a waiting-gentlewoman; the letter in 2.3 is from 'a dish of skim milk;' he'd like to 'brain him with his lady's fan.' 'This is no world,' says Hotspur, 'to play with mammets and to tilt with lips,'—women's games.

Use the images that other people apply to you. Westmorland says (1.1.96):

> This is his uncle's teaching...
> Which makes him prune himself, and bristle up
> The crest of youth against your dignity.

By looking in the notes you will discover that this is the image of a hawk preening its topknot. The hawk is a hunter, wild, unpredictable and badtempered: a noble bird, but when ruffled slightly absurd like all birds. Perhaps this is how Hotspur reacts when irritated, both physically and mentally. Look at Northumberland's

> ... what a wasp-stung and impatient fool
> Art thou to break into this woman's mood... (1.3.236)

If you practice saying Hotspur's lines in this scene as if you were literally stung by a wasp, all sorts of interesting feelings and gestures will occur to you. Think about the King's epithet: 'Mars in swathling clothes' (3.2.112). Imagine the fierce god of war swaddled up like a baby. Hotspur's youth makes his pigheaded bellicosity both foolish and touching; this could be an important element in your performance.

Don't rush apologetically over the *classical references*. They may have faded down the centuries and seem lifeless and cumbrous, but to Shakespeare and his audience they were a mark of sparkling literacy. Think of them as a fashionable vocabulary, a kind of educated slang, but still with some of the force of their elemental origins in the vast events of life, the cycle of the seasons, day and night, birth, copulation and death. To the Renaissance Englishman, Mars was not just the planetary home of little green men, nor merely a handsome helmeted statue. He was nearer to the ancient personification of rage and rivalry which goads men to war, bloodshed and death. You can't be expected to *act* all that, of course, but by being aware of the powers pent in the image you will re-mint them for your audience.

Expletives and Exclamations

Hotspur swears a lot: good mouth-filling oaths. Use them forcibly. Remember that the devil had more power *c* 1600 than he has today, and oaths more gusto and shock-value. Elizabethans sometimes held bad-language competitions. Hotspur uses zounds, sblood, God save the mark, a plague upon't, plenty of Os, Has Hos, God's mes, etc. Don't forget that you are in competition with the rich expletives of Falstaff and Hal (see 2.4.495ff).

Don't be skimpy with your Os. Think of them literally as ciphers: blank spaces left in the text for you to fill in for yourself with a gut-sound. Try out all the ways of saying 'O' you can think of; the possibilities are infinite. What do you suppose Shakespeare would have liked to hear an actor convey with:

> O! let the hours be short
> Till fields and blows and groans applaud our sport!
> *(1 Hen IV* 1.3.302)

or

> O Harry! thou hast robbed me of my youth! (5.4.77)

or

> O! I could prophesy! (5.4.83)

or

> **Macduff** Your royal father's murdered.
> **Malcolm**   O! by whom?
> *(Macb* 2.3.107)

SUPPORTING ROLES

Many characters, especially in the early plays, are not as richly stocked with clues as Hotspur and you'll have to work your imagination harder. Or to take an example from a later play; suppose you are Lady Macduff. (a) The facts: you are Macduff's wife and mother of an unspecified number of children. (b) Other people's comments: Ross's description of her as 'murdered deer' (4.3) and her husband's 'What! all my pretty chickens and their dam?' (c) Character details: very general. She is emotional and tough-spirited in the way she speaks, but there is nothing particular about her. (d) First appearance: frightened. (e) Humour: minimal. (f) Detective work: there are two images in the scene that have to do with birds as victims (the deer and the pretty chickens are also slaughtered creatures):

> the poor wren,
> The most diminutive of birds will fight—
> Her young ones in her nest—against the owl.
>
> (4.2.9)

and:

> **Lady Macduff** How will you live?
> **Boy** As birds do, mother.
> **Lady Macduff** ... Poor bird! thoudst never fear the net nor lime,
> The pit-fall nor the gin ...
>
> (4.2.31)

These images give you a clue: you might think of Lady Macduff as a trapped bird. Perhaps at the Globe she was played by the small boy who did Celia, Hermia and Maria, the 'youngest wren of nine'. Imagine a bird in its nest, eyes darting, breathing quickly, shrill and savage when the predator swoops. Most important, there is nothing sentimental about birds. They only seem frail and pathetic to human beings. There should be nothing winsome about either Lady Macduff or her precocious son. Though Shakespeare (like some film directors) blatantly used children to bring a lump to his audience's throat, Elizabethan children were like small adults. If you look closely at their exchange, you'll see that it's quite racy and brutal.

If you are stuck with a smallish part—Benvolio, say, or Mrs Quickly or Northumberland in the *Henry IV*s—try to find some eccentricity to define yourself entertainingly for the audience. This is not to suggest that you resort to a twitch or a false nose or a funny walk, or anything irrelevant and silly. Something as visually simple as a pair of spectacles for Benvolio, for example, which he could take off and polish now and then in a vague, swottish way, will help to particularize and vivify him. Better still, look for mental eccentricities, making sure there is justification for them in the text. Falstaff apostrophizes Mrs Quickly as 'Dame Partlet the hen', and this might suggest to the actress a fussy, pecking, feathery way of both looking and thinking. For

Northumberland, you might decide that he has not a shred of a sense of humour, as the text shows. Think of how everyone in the real world has some quality that is their own; stage characters should not be any different, in fact their personal quirks must be loud and clear in order to register with an audience. There should be no such thing as a 'straight' performance from any member of the company.

Some characters have no clues at all. Suppose you are a Divers Lord, or the Second Son of Sir Rowland de Boys (*AYL* 5.4). You are justified in inventing all the circumstances you like in order to bring yourself to life, within decorous limits, of course. If you are a real actor, you will do this automatically; you would never walk on stage merely to mouth lines. You will always be someone, coming from somewhere.

LOCATION AND PROPS

Performers have sometimes been led astray by the nebulously located places in the plays. In the literal-minded eighteenth and nineteenth centuries this vagueness was regarded as evidence of poor playwrighting and was compensated for with vast, historically exact sets which took ages to change. Shakespeare productions in this century have reverted to the simple, mobile staging of the Elizabethan theatre (see Chapter 3) and so the onus of scene setting is now back where it began, in the words.

It is up to you to place yourself imaginatively, using the clues in the text. Don't rely on anything the director or designer may be cooking up for the first night in the way of suggestive decor or strategic lighting. From the first rehearsal you must be as specific and particular in your own mind about your ambiance as about the facts of your life and character. Again, a good actor will be this instinctively. Some people nowadays are not used to working their visual imaginations, and may need help from books or discussions.

The name of the place you are in is not literally significant; what matters is how it affects your thoughts. Sometimes Shakespeare provides plenty of information; in *Rom & Jul* 2.2 there is darkness, a summer evening, an orchard with walls that are high and hard to climb, fruit trees whose tops are tipped with silver moonlight, a pomegranate tree and a light shining from Juliet's window. In the first two ghost scenes in *Hamlet* there are: a freezing midnight, stars, a distant high hill visible at dawn, a cock crowing (presumably from the livestock quarters), noise of revelry, possibly a moon and nearby a terrible cliff falling to the roaring sea. Shakespeare knew that weathers, heat and cold, light and dark affect the imagination powerfully, and the briefest clue is enough to stimulate a whole imagined world. Zeffirelli's stage production of *Rom & Jul* was saturated in the effluences of Benvolio's 'The day is hot . . .' Lines like the following perform their scene-setting function more effectively than the most elaborate stage or film setting in the world:

Prologue From camp to camp, through the foul womb of night
The hum of either army stilly sounds,
That the fixed sentinels almost receive
The secret whispers of each other's watch.
(*Hen V* 4)
Gloucester Alack, the night comes on and the high winds
Do sorely ruffle; for many miles about
There's scarce a bush.
(*Lear* 2.4)
Brutus Get you to bed again, it is not day.
Is not tomorrow, boy, the ides of March?
. . . The exhalations, whizzing in the air,
Give so much light that I may read by them.
(*Jul C* 2.1)

If there are no clues, locate yourself firmly and simply in your own invented setting, discussing it if you like with your fellow actors. Have natural, specific actions *if you need them*. Lady Macduff, for example, could sit in a room in her draughty Fifeshire castle; you could imagine a vast fireplace, swaying tapestries and mice in the wainscot. You could caress the boy, or just hold him protectively. Let your actions occur naturally from your thoughts and surroundings, and don't do anything fussy or complicated. Even if you are a faceless lord or an anonymous spear-carrier your sense of location should be no less specific. When everyone on stage is imaginatively placed in a setting, the scene will acquire realistic depth and solidity.

In a large part it will help to chart your positions; here is a location plan for Hotspur:

1. 1.3 Chez the King of London. A public room, because the King exits *from* Hotspur and company; a place where people behave formally.
2. 2.3 Hotspur's own territory, daytime. (Shakespeare does not name Warkworth, though this was where Hotspur lived historically.) He is at ease, can order his wife and servants around.
3. 3.1 A general room chez Glendower, night time, presumably in Wales, a long way from Warkworth. Hotspur is not behaving well, and clearly does not feel awed by his surroundings.
4. 4.1 Unspecified. Near Shrewsbury. Might be interior, a tent or a barn, or else an open space. Decide which. If outside, describe the lie of the land to yourself.
5. 4.2 Ditto. Daytime.
6. 5.2 Day of the battle. Windy and blustery. If Hotspur is addressing his troops ('Let each man do his best') the scene must be outdoors.
7. 5.3 The Battlefield. Noise? Smoke? Terrain?
8. 5.4 The Battlefield. How does the setting change, in your own mind, between 7 and 8?

If you handle props let them be as real to you as possible, even if they're papier mâché. Remember how rare and expensive such things as paper and glass were, in fact all domestic objects; how laboriously everything was welded, embroidered, worked by hand. Your sword would have been as important to you as your car key is today (and far more difficult to replace). Feel the weight and reality of everything you touch.

Once your performance is rooted in real things, your invention can begin to soar. The more poetry and passion the part demands, the more fundamentally real you must be; you can't achieve the heights of a Lear or an Othello without bulding a solid imaginative foundation.

BIG ACTING

Shakespeare needs big acting. In the Elizabethan playhouses the audience sat around three sides of a projecting stage. Like spectators at a boxing match they were close to the actors; every twitch, every blink, every bead of sweat must have been visible. It would be hard to let your attention wander from those faces and voices, and not unlike watching actors on a big cinema screen. Unfortunately there are very few theatres now where actors are magnified by sheer proximity to the audience.

There is evidence in the writings of the times to show that Elizabethans and Jacobeans probably talked more and louder than we do; gesticulated, wept, laughed, kissed and embraced more freely, and generally expressed themselves more extrovertly and passionately, both on and off stage. The colourless gentility of Puritanism had not yet subdued people's spontaneity. Twentieth-century behaviour is of thinner stuff. Think how in the last fifty years even small gestures like touching or raising the hat have almost disappeared (along with hats). Bows, curtsies, hand-kissing, etc, are now quaintly antiquated. Everyone now wears fairly uniform clothes regardless of sex or profession, which are cheap and easy and unrestricting. Social behaviour is undemonstrative, except in peculiar situations like football matches and political demonstrations. Rhetoric, style and manners are no longer desirable adjuncts to social behaviour, and professional actors have had to reduce the scale of their acting to accommodate the small eye of the TV camera. One outcome of all this is that in many Shakespeare productions the play seems to hang limply on small, slovenly performances. Actors need to find a way of filling out the roles in a way which is both true to the text and acceptable to a modern audience.

Big acting has a lot to do with confidence. Imagine yourself to be taller, more graceful, more electrifying than (perhaps) you are. Think of what will interest your audience; be eager to flatter their intelligence, reach out to them with your thoughts and abilities. All this must be done tactfully. Your natural desire for admiration (which is what makes you want to act) should be expressed in whatever way is most entertaining. You must be conceited and considerate at the same time. And you must never be unreal.

There are simple technical aids to big acting. Relaxation is, of course, the key to confidence (see Appendix). It is important to use your voice in the right way, and this is discussed in the next chapter. It is also important to feel that you look attractive or at least interesting, which is why actors should always have the final word about costume and hair arrangement. Think detachedly about your best physical points: how can you use them with the right effect for your part? Remember that the Globe actors were accomplished fencers, dancers and riders. Some exercises:

(a) Strong leg muscles are important; you need to rest on them firmly and relaxedly, like a boxer. If your legs are weak, do ten slow knee-bends daily. With feet slightly apart, hands on hips, rise on your toes, support yourself as long as possible by imagining a straight post at your back; don't tense; sink *slowly* to a squat, bounce gently once or twice; rise again slowly to your toes; relax. Or you could try running up and down stairs.

(b) A straight spine, relaxed neck and steady head make an enormous difference to height. Strengthen your spine with this exercise: make yourself into an armadillo shape by resting on hands and knees, dropping the head and arching the back: from the topmost vertebra in the neck to the end of your tail you should feel like a bent bow. Now, slowly, bend the other way; raise the head and tail and make your back into a saddle. Feel your spine easing gently into position. Finally, straighten it so that it is parallel to the floor. You should look like a table on straight legs.

(c) If you can, find a few minutes alone in the place where you'll be performing. Stand centre stage, face front and imagine the auditorium full of people. Spread your arms wide as if you were embracing them all. Pretend you're an old-fashioned Hollywood star. Imagine an invisible web of wires running from your fingers, the top of your head and your feet, joining you to each person in the audience. Now turn sideways, walk about, sit down; keep thinking about the wires.

(d) Say 'O gentlemen! the time of life is short' (or any line you like) conversationally to yourself. Repeat it to an imaginary person sitting beside you. Now try it on an invisible critic in the front row, on someone in the centre, and then on someone at the back of the auditorium, or in the gods (if you have them). Finally, say the line to a huge listening crowd somewhere beyond the theatre walls. Don't strain. Each time you should feel a physical change in your body, and a wider stretching of your spirit. Try to stretch your whole performance as far as that listening crowd.

ENERGY AND SEXUALITY

These are important aspects of big acting. Performers often underestimate the amount of energy needed for Shakespeare. You need, at least, to reciprocate the titanic effort which went into the creation of the plays.

A few minutes' physical warm-up before rehearsal, dancing to a record or singing will work wonders. If people show signs of flagging, make them lie down on the floor, relax from top to toe and listen to some music or a soothing poem. The company will be energetic if they are interested and happy.

The powerful sexuality of many roles and situations is often underplayed or entirely ignored, although it is often the key to a vivid production, particularly of a comedy. Shakespeare is the most sensual of writers. Whatever kind of sexuality is expressed by your character, whether romantic (Romeo), sensual (Troilus), embittered (Hamlet), funny (Audrey), disgusted (Thersites) or crude (Launce), or any other kind, use all the references with enjoyment. Many are implicit or figurative. Take Juliet's reference to the wind-swift Cupid's wings (2.5.8). Cupid is instantly associated in the listener's mind with love, and especially erotic love; wings suggest flying and swiftness and are mentioned several times in this play. But more particularly the actress might think of the fluttering, the breathless, light headed nature of sexual excitement which is symbolized by Cupid's wings; and she might be reminded of the arrows, which signify the sweet-sour pains of love and love-making. Sex, as Shakespeare knew, is an interesting and urgent matter to everyone, and a vital ingredient of good theatre.

Speeches for practising sexual passion: Juliet: 'Gallop apace...' (*Rom & Jul* 3.2). Troilus: 'And suddenly...' (*Tr & Cr* 4.3), Benedick: 'This can be no trick...' (*Much Ado* 2.3.239), and Olivia: 'What is your parentage...' (*Twel N* 1.5.310).

Performers should be encouraged to use energy and sexual imagination from the beginning of rehearsals. They will not be shy to do so if everyone does so. Here are some ice-breaking, de-inhibiting games which may help:
(a) Get everyone to stand close together and imagine they are all trapped in a stuck tube train. They are all foreign and no-one understands anyone else.

(b) Think of a simple story that everyone knows, like the Three Bears. Divide the company into groups and allot parts. Ask each group to perform the story in a different way: as a ballet, or a Noh play, as if at the Globe, or in a Western, or an old-fashioned musical, or a Coward play, etc. You could hold a competition between the different groups.
(c) Perform a ten-minute version of your play as a silent film.
(d) Perform a scene as grand opera.

STYLE

Clearly, in a Shakespeare play you can't behave exactly like a twentieth-century person; the words won't let you. As you create your character, you should also think about manners and attitudes and movement (these, very broadly, being the constituents of style), anchoring yourself on the information in the text, and using your historical imagination. Style is also an expression of individuality, and you need every ounce of that for a Shakespearian role. 'Style', says Michel St Denis sternly in his book on the subject,* 'is liberation from the mud of naturalism.'

Here are some points of verbal and physical style to look out for:

(a) Thou and You

Mark the 'thou' and 'yous' in your play and think about why they are used and to whom. They are often helpful pointers to mental attitudes. When Proteus and Valentine are friends in *Two Gent* 1.1 and 2.4 they address each other as 'thou'; but in Act 2 when they are shy and restrained they use 'you'. Imogen in *Cymb* 1.6 expresses her opinion of Iachimo first with contemptuous 'thous' and later reverts to a formal 'you'.

(b) Appellations and Titles

It is easy to use these automatically as if they were no more than Christian names. Today you wouldn't hear a girl greeting her husband with 'O my good lord', or a man calling his friend's wife 'my most sacred lady', nor someone addressing his chairman as 'my liege'. Think about the social and mental attitudes implied in these vocatives.

* *Theatre: The Rediscovery of Style* (Heinemann 1960)

(c) Movement

If you are wearing Elizabethan clothes you will need to practise in the clothes bowing, curtseying, sitting down, running and going through doorways (women), and also dancing, fighting and dressing or undressing (armour, for instance). There is more about the wearing of costume in Chapter 8.

(d) Bows and Curtseys

Don't skimp on bows and curtseys, both because they were part of life and because audiences always enjoy them. If you make an obeisance don't just do it because the director tells you to. Think about the hierarchy of Tudor times and your place in it. You knelt to your superior because you believed that he/she *was* superior; a bow has primitive origins in fear, and its courteous significance came later. If you are Hotspur, or Richard III, you can of course use obeisances to express the opposite of courtesy by performing them off-handedly. Women curtsied by bending both knees and inclining the head, with the hands relaxed on the side of the dress. Men should stand with legs apart and one foot forward and bow from the waist, while sweeping off their hats and bending slightly at the knees.

(e) Kisses and Embraces

These convey both style and character. Formal kisses on either cheek can be used by both men and women, as among modern royalty. Men should be free about hugging one another and kissing ladies' hands (formally) or wrists, or (informally) lips; Cressida is 'kissed in general' on the lips by a crowd of (to her) completely strange Greeks.

(f) Gestures

Shakespeare's actors probably used more gestures and performed them more boldly and broadly than would seem natural today. It is likely, too, that they had a repertoire of rhetorical movements, such as putting a hand on the heart to show love. Every schoolboy was taught the art of rhetoric, and perhaps the gestures too. Their conscious use is now almost obsolete, except in ballet or mime, though clergymen, politicians and people on soap boxes sometimes use rhetorical gestures quite spontaneously. There is an interesting approach to this aspect of stagecraft in Bertram Joseph's *Elizabethan Acting* (OUP, ed 1964).

Gestures must never be made vacuously, or for elegance or mere visual effect. They should be definite and either emphasize or illustrate what you're saying. It is helpful to study the internal evidence of Elizabethan stage behaviour. Try to perform the actions described below firstly as you imagine a Globe actor would perform them, and then in a way that would be truthful and interesting to a modern audience:

> Nor do not saw the air too much with your hand,
> thus, but use it all gently...
>
> *Hamlet* 3.2.4.
>
> *The Queen returns, finds the King dead and makes passionate action.*
>
> 3.2.156.
>
> ... once me thought
> It lifted up its head and did address
> Itself to motion, like as it would speak.
>
> 1.2.215

Hor. It beckons you to go away with it,
As if it some impartment did desire
To you alone.
Mar. Look, with what a courteous action
It waves you to a more removed ground.

> 1.4.58
>
> That you, at such times seeing me, never shall,
> With arms encumber'd thus, or this headshake... to note
> That you know aught of me.
>
> 1.5.173
>
> He took me by the wrist and held me hard,
> Then goes he to the length of all his arm,
> And, with his other hand thus o'er his brow,
> He falls to such perusal of my face
> As he would draw it. Long stayed he so;
> At last, a little shaking of mine arm,
> And thrice his head thus waving up and down,
> He raised a sigh so piteous and profound...
>
> 2.1.87

What! man; ne'er pull your hat upon your brows;
Give sorrow words...

Macb. 4.3.208

> ... yesternight at supper
> You suddenly arose, and walked about
> Musing and sighing, with your arms across,
> And when I asked you what the matter was,
> You stared upon me with ungentle looks.
> I urged you further; then you scratched your head,
> And too impatiently stamped with your foot;
> Yet I insisted, yet you answered not,
> But, with an angry wafture of your hand,
> Gave sign for me to leave you.
>
> *Jul C* 2.1.238

A very useful, short book on style and movement is *Playing Period Plays* by Lyn Oxenford (Part II: Elizabethan and Jacobean Period) (J. G. Miller, 1957).

PLAYING THE WOMEN'S PARTS

Shakespeare wrote his young women's roles for boys with unbroken voices, who were trained while being attached to an adult player as a kind of apprentice-cum-batman. It is clear from Puritan anathema on the subject that the boys made very convincing girls, with a subtle allure for both sexes; and Shakespeare further complicated their equivocal appeal in no less than five plays, by having them dress as girl-boys, or in Rosalind's case as a girl-boy pretending to be a girl.

An actress does not have the same quality as a boy dressed as a girl. But if you think about your role with the qualities and limitations of boy-players in mind you will make some interesting discoveries.

Begin by imagining what it is like to inhabit a boy's body; think about how he stands, walks, holds his arms, where his best muscles are, how he looks out at the world, and so on. Imagine yourself as a boy on a playhouse stage in a ruff, stomacher and farthingale (see Fig 27). You will find that specifically feminine movements of the waist and hips are restricted, so that you have to rely on the expressiveness of your face, head, hands and feet. You will discover that a boy is more firmly planted on the earth than a girl; he has bigger feet, narrower hips and a longer stride. Generally speaking, his energies are more active and outgoing and confident. His horizons tend to be wider. Compare the range of Rosalind's imagination—as manifested in her references to such exotic diversities as Turks, Ethiops, the South Seas, the Bay of Portugal, apes, parrots, Troilus, Leander, etc—with that of, for example, Hedda Gabler. Even the most gentle women like Cordelia, Marina, Desdemona and Miranda have a wiriness and directness, or some quality that acts as an antidote to mere prettiness and goodness. Cordelia, for instance, takes a sharp line with her sisters (*Lear* 1.1.271); Desdemona has a practical, rather tactless side to her nature (*Oth* 3.3).

Only a few of Shakespeare's women are prone to conventional female failings such as garrulousness and vacillation, and they are generally older: the Nurse, Mrs Quickly and Valeria, for example. Perhaps these parts were designed for adult men and played for quite broad, 'camp' effects, rather like pantomime dames.

For more on the subject, see Granville-Barker's Preface to *Ant & Cl*, and *Shakespeare's Boy Actors* by W Robertson Davies (Dent, 1939).

5 Speaking the Text

Actors are sometimes hypnotized by the fact that the plays are in verse, and think they should produce a special incantatory warble, an I-am-speaking-Shakespeare voice. This is nonsense. Another mistake is to think that if you speak slowly (as to foolish foreigners) you are more likely to be understood. This is no more true in the theatre than it is in real life. The worst mistake of all is to imagine that you will somehow clarify your text if you ignore the verse and use a casual twentieth-century-conversational tone; the chances are that you will be quite unintelligible.

The verse itself imposes a range of problems. Compare these passages, the first from the early *Mids N*, the second from *Ant & Cl* (*c* 1606):

Helena   O! I am out of breath in this fond chase,
The more my prayer, the lesser is my grace,
Happy is Hermia, wheresoe'er she lies;
For she hath blessed and attractive eyes.
How came her eyes so bright? not with salt tears;
If so, my eyes are oftener washed than hers.
No, no, I am as ugly as a bear;
For beasts that meet me run away for fear;
Therefore no marvel though Demetrius
Do as a monster fly my presence thus.   (2.2)

Cleopatra Lead me from hence;
I faint. O Iras! Charmian! 'Tis no matter.
Go to the fellow, good Alexas; bid him
Report the feature of Octavia, her years,
Her inclination, let him not leave out
The colour of her hair; bring me word quickly.
Let him forever go: let him not—Charmian!
Though he be painted one way like a Gorgon,
The other way's a Mars. Bid you Alexas
Bring me word how tall she is. Pity me, Charmian,
But do not speak to me. Lead me to my chamber.
   (2.5)

The fairly regular metre of the early plays evolved into a compact, broken verse, which is often indistinguishable from natural speech. Helena's speech rhymes, and the thoughts pause at the end of each line with the punctuation, except for the somewhat hiccuping leap between 'Demetrius' and 'do'. It is easy to lapse into a warble or at best a monotonous sing-song. Cleopatra's lines are also arranged in pentameters but they are far from iambic, and they often halt halfway. The pauses of thought happen all over the place. Here you have the opposite problem: of sustaining a rhythm while you unravel the layers of meaning and emotion for the audience.

There is no such thing as a correct Shakespearian delivery, any more than there is a right way to say good morning. How well or badly you speak Shakespeare depends on how imaginatively you respond to the content of your speeches; and this depends on how concentratedly you rivet yourself to their thought sequences. When a performance is criticized because the 'poetry was missing' it does not mean that the actors failed to warble or observe their end stops. It means that they were not ascending to the brightest heaven of Shakespeare's invention: that they were failing as interpreters.

This chapter does not propose to interpret Shakespeare to you. But it does suggest that close attention to the physical shape of your text, especially the line-endings and punctuation, will help you to understand and speak it as Shakespeare wanted it spoken. It will also help with memorization. Gradually you will discover that the metrical form of your lines is a marvellous scaffolding designed especially to support you, the performer.

USING THE VERSE STRUCTURE

There is information to be gained about the verse-speaking simply by looking at your text on the page. Why is the fact that it is in iambic pentameters important to you, the actor? The literary history of blank verse is not relevant here. In practical terms, the pentameter is versatile; it occupies a good length in time for both speaker and listener; it is neither too short and jerky like a quatrain:

> The fox, the ape and the humble bee

nor too long (like a hexameter) for the breath or the listener's memory:

> Then death rock me asleep, abridge my doleful days.

Because the stress is so variable the voice is not tempted to jog soporifically, and because the midway pause, the caesura, is mobile the line does not tend to collapse into two segments. A pentameter imposes on the speaking voice a good balance of discipline and freedom, and is the best verse for imitating natural speech.

It makes sense, therefore, to allow your voice to be supported by the pentameters like a surf board on the ocean. You should adjust your pulse to the powerful forward impetus of the writing, surging with the lines and resting when they rest. Resting is not the same as stopping (a play should not stop until the audience has finished applauding). A rest might be described as a dynamic silence in the sound track of your speech. There are different sorts of rest with different sorts of dynamism:

(a) *Line endings.* You must mark the end of each pentameter, otherwise your speaking will lack the beautiful intrinsic pentametrical tautness. When there is no end punctuation, the rest is barely discernible; imagine it as a tiny penflourish on the last letter of the line.

(b) *The Caesura.* Sometimes there is a rest which may or may not be punctuated in the middle of a pentameter. It can have a useful function, eg, dividing an antithesis or a balance:

> The sum is paid: the traitors are agreed. (*Hen V* Prol. 2.33)

or a change of thought:

> Perchance she cannot meet him: that's not so (*Rom & Jul* 2.5.3)

But the important point about a caesura rest is that it does *not* mark the end of the line; it must suggest more to come.

(c) *Punctuation marks.* It is generally agreed that the Folio punctuation can be read as a fairly consistent code of instructions to the actor. Commas, colons, semicolons and full stops represent rests of increasing length, nearly (but not exactly) the equivalent of modern marks. Capitalized words carry a slight emphasis. In most editions the Folio punctuation has been updated and adjusted to direct the eye of the reader rather than the voice of the speaker. You may find it interesting to refer to the original punctuation, and to discover which words are capitalized and to note subtle differences in meaning. (For a detailed review of Folio punctuation see *Shakespearian Punctuation* by P Simpson (OUP, 1911, reprinted 1969).)

Weight-Words

If you know that you're going to rest on—or rather after—a word, you will automatically give it weight. For a small second you will make it vibrate memorably in your listener's ear. Thus the strongest-positioned words in blank verse are those at the end of each line, or half line, or before each punctuation mark, especially a full stop. Shakespeare nearly always uses these positions for important words, and by doing so he encourages the actor to release a modicum of extra energy at the end of each sentence or phrase, and so to *think through* his lines (a basic essential of technique). He also keeps the audience's collective ear in a state of alert anticipation, waiting for the weight-word. This is one of the reasons why the verse has such tremendous, irresistible impetus, and why—once you have locked your own energies into the energy of the lines—it is so exhilarating to speak Shakespeare. Of course you should not just prong the weight-words mechanically with your voice; having understood the reasons for their weight, you should *think* them more emphatically. Your voice will then stress instinctively.

Why, for example, are the weight-words important in this passage?

> How oft when men are at the point of *death*,
> Have they been *merry*? Which their keepers call/
> A lightning before *death*? Oh how may *I*
> Call this a *lightning*?
>
> (*Rom & Jul* 5.3.88)

Death is obviously the enormous presence at this moment of the play. The muffled monosyllabic sound is repeated twice in three lines, and emphasized even more by its juxtaposition to the light, living sounds of 'merry' and 'lightning'. 'Call' is a brief end-stop, which has the effect of putting 'a lightning before death' into inverted commas. Shakespeare also draws your attention to the *I*, not an obvious stress, but a powerful, agonized, isolating one.

At some point you should go through your lines marking the iambic *scansion* quite mechanically: de-DUM de-DUM de-DUM de-DUM de-DUM:

'Once *more* un*to* the *breach* dear *friends* once *more*'

Of course many—perhaps most—of Shakespeare's lines are not spoken in this regular way. Quite often the first foot becomes a trochee:

Now is the *wint*er *of* our dis*cont*ent

or an iamb may be reversed to special effect:

And *by* op*pos*ing *end* them? To *die*, to *sleep*.

An extra 'feminine' ending is sometimes added:

When *it* did *taste* the *worm*wood *on* the *nip*ple

or a syllable may be missing, indicating a pause:

Must *give* us *pause. There*'s the res*pect*

or sometimes a line defies all attempts at iamabic confinement:

Nor *rain*, *wind*, *thund*er, *fire*, are my *daugh*ters.

However, if you are not sure of the sense or the most effective stress of a line, the *theoretical* pattern often provides insight, either by helping you to simplify or by showing where and why Shakespeare has altered the iambic rhythm. Take these lines:

Sir, *you* and *I* must *part*, but *that*'s not *it*:
Sir, *you* and *I* have *loved*, but *there*'s not *it*;
That *you* know *well*: some*thing* it *is* I *would*—
O! *my* ob*liv*ion *is* a *very* *Ant*ony,
And *I* am *all* for*got*ten.

Iambically speaking, the two 'sirs' are short. But you might decide that Shakespeare has reversed the first foot:

Sir, you and *I* must *part*

thus making the 'you' short and pushing you to land quite weightily on the 'I': a useful stress for an egotistical reading of Cleopatra (the 'I' in the fifth line is also marked). You could linger on the 'sir' lovingly, or doubtfully, or ironically, or however. On the other hand, you could stick to the light stress on the 'sirs' and dwell on the regular 'you' and 'I' and 'part', in which case the 'sir' is a throw-away, almost an 'er' sound; this is a more hesitant, and subtly more generous reading of the line. You might also make valuable use of the iambic weight on 'all' in the fifth line, to convey the wide, doleful expanse of her forgetfulness.

By stressing the weight-words you sustain the shape and forward drive of the verse. You may also want to stress words which are not drawn to your attention by the structure or the Folio punctuation. This is up to your artistic judgement. When in doubt, economize. An audience's ear is selective; you will help its concentration by picking out a path of key words. A richly poetic passage may seem to offer an impossible choice:

> Yet I'll not shed her blood,
> Nor scar that whiter skin of hers, then Snow,
> And smooth as Monumental Alablaster:
>
> (*Oth* 5.2.3, Folio version)

Should you go for the verbs, the adjectives, the alliterative words? The weight-words, blood, snow, alablaster, economically invoke the potent sensuousness of the thought: life, death, redness, whiteness, heat, cold, smoothness, flesh, stone and effigies: they are all—and more—there in those three words. You could use the 'whiter' and 'smooth' for underlining. Notice also that the capitalization prods you to linger on the soft labials of Monumental Alablaster, which raises the question of

USING THE SOUNDS

Without lapsing into a Poetry Voice you should be alert to Shakespeare's verbal sound effects. There are more in some plays and characters than in others, and they should be embodied into your character as truthfully and specifically as you absorb its other details (see pp 37–42). Listen, for example, to the onomatopoeia of the first line in the following, and the rushing, windy, fricative fs and ws:

> Gallop apace, you fiery footed steeds,
> Towards Phoebus' lodging; such a Wagoner
> As Phaeton would whip you to the west...
>
> (*Rom & Jul* 3.2.1)

You will need your acutest awareness of the power and pleasure of sounds (see note on articulation below).

Don't be self-conscious about *rhymes*. They too are pleasurable. Where there are many, in early plays such as the *Dream*, they help to propel the verse by making your audience's ear anticipate the rhyme word. Otherwise they are always used to some precise effect, of formality, for example, or of climax:

> Ring the alarm bell! Blow wind! Come wrack!
> At least we'll die with harness on our back!
>
> *(Macb* 5.5)

The second rhyme word should carry more weight, or your climax will fizzle out on you.

Rhetorical Figures

Every Elizabethan schoolboy learned the art of rhetoric, a necessary skill in a world of verbal communication. But there is no need to agonize over the figures or even to learn their sesquipedalian names in order to recognize them. Simply enjoy them: their cleverness, their memorability and formal pleasure:

> Thy name well fits thy faith, thy faith thy name
>
> *(Cymb* 4.2.381)
>
> And let the kettle to the trumpet speak,
> The trumpet to the cannoneer without,
> The cannons to the heavens, the heavens to earth...
>
> *(Ham* 5.2.289)

See *Acting Shakespeare* by B L Joseph (Routledge, 1960) for more on rhetoric.

Some Technical Reminders

(a) **Rising inflections.** It is easy to run out of energy before the end of a pentameter or a punctuated sentence, and let your voice slide down wearily. Your audience's interest will droop with it. The exclamation marks of modern editions are misleading in this respect, because they tend to make you drop rather than raise your inflection:

> Oh what a rogue and peasant slave am I!

The Folio has a question mark here, to indicate a questioning-like rise for the voice, rather like a Welsh accent, or certain types of American. This would probably have been quite a natural inflection for Burbage and Co.

(b) **Launching out.** Do not slide tentatively into a play or a scene or a speech. Shakespeare usually gives you some strong interesting sounds to attack with. If a scene begins in *medias res* make your audience feel that they are interrupting something:

> Nay, but this dotage of our general's
> O'erflows the measure... *Ant & Cl*
>
> O for a muse of fire... *Hen V*
>
> Hung be the heavens with black... *1 Hen VI*

(c) Seize on the *apostrophes and exclamations* boldly. Actors are often shy of these and mumble them feebly as if wishing they weren't there, but used with conviction they can be exciting:

> Gallop apace, you fiery footed steeds...

Juliet should loudly address the horses of the sun; for the moment they are there, moving too slowly. Similarly, Hamlet's

> O all you host of heaven! O earth! What else?
> And shall I couple hell?

is not just a big gorblimey but an invocation to the goodness above, or perhaps the evil below, to the visible world, in fact to everything in Hamlet's universe. It should have urgent actuality.

(d) *Lists*, like speeches and scenes, should mount steadily and not be trotted out in a monotone; practise with *Tr & Cr* 4.4.33 and 5.1.153. If each word carries a little more weight than the one before it, the list will be propelled forward.

AUDIBILITY AND ARTICULATION

If you can't be heard by an audience there is not much point in appearing on a stage. In a Shakespeare play you must not only be audible, you must be *easy* to listen to. This means finding the proper *volume* and level of projection for wherever you're going to perform. It is up to the director to tell you if you can't be heard, or if you're bawling uncomfortably. It is very helpful to spend half an hour or so practising levels on your own in the area where you'll be performing. Think of your voice as an object which you are throwing to each member of the audience; your aim must be accurate; the audience mustn't have to make the slightest effort to catch what you say.

Tone and Resonance

Not speaking loud enough is not the only cause of inaudibility. If you have a strained, breathy or monotonous voice the audience will soon stop listening to you. Voices which are easiest to listen to are produced by breath drawn from the base of the lungs and not obstructed by tensions in the throat or ugly nasal resonance (see further explanation and exercises in the Appendix). You can't really relax until you are breathing properly, and you can't be creative unless you relax.

Another cause of inaudibility is bad *articulation*. Hamlet is talking precisely about this when he tells the Players to 'Speak the speech, I pray you, as I pronounced it to you, trippingly on the tongue; but if you mouth it, as many of your players do, I had as lief the town-crier spoke my lines.' (3.2)

The point of this advice—and notice that Hamlet gives it priority—is that words which are shaped with precision and energy by the tongue and lips are far more interesting to listen to than words which are slopped out, or emitted as loud, symbolic sounds. The town-crier's function is merely to produce a reassuring wail; but a Shakespearian actor has to convey extremely complicated thoughts and shades of emotion, and your mouth is where this complexity is made physical. Also, proper muscular articulation is pleasurable, an advanced version of happy sensations like suckling and kissing.

There is nothing mystical about the practise of good articulation, which is simply a matter of limbering up the muscles of the mouth and using them properly. Good professional actors do regular articulation exercises, as ballet dancers do bar exercises.

Hamlet's speech to the Players is the best and most succinct acting manual ever written. It should be engraved in gold on every student-actor's diploma. He says in essence: articulate properly, be natural, don't do too much and don't do too little. These are the fundamentals. Where you go from there depends on you and Shakespeare.

6 Fights and Battles

GENERAL POINTS

There are fights of one kind or another in nineteen of the thirty-seven plays. Some fights (in, eg *1 Hen VI* or *AYL*) may have been included as much for their spectacular value as for the part they play in the plot, like fights in epic and gangster films. It has been suggested that there was a fine (and precocious) swordsman in the company, who played La Pucelle and later Tybalt, Douglas, Laertes, Edmund, etc. Fights and battles often provide the denouement (eg in *1 Hen IV*, *Ham*). They are an important consideration for Shakespeare performers.

Most people enjoy watching a fight. The Elizabethans, more primitive than twentieth-century people in this respect, liked seeing bears being whipped and bulls baited to death by dogs, and for a special treat a good hanging, drawing and quartering. Like many people today, they enjoyed crude and cruel representations of death. The theatre world was often the focus of violent goings-on; Ben Jonson only just escaped being hanged for murdering Gabriel Spenser, a fellow player, and Marlowe was stabbed to death through the head in a Deptford tavern. Men wore swords and carried shields or bucklers (the latter at least until the 1580s) as a matter of course. Shakespeare left his sword in his will to a Mr Thomas Combe of Stratford. Your personal safety depended on what weapon you carried and how well you used it.

To the Elizabethans, sword fighting was both a necessary means of defence and a sport. It had a disreputable side and a fashionable side; it was studied as an art and used as a way of settling arguments. Conservatives favoured the traditional British broad sword against the fiendish foreign rapier, which was introduced during the first half of the sixteenth century from Spain and Italy. The clash between the two points of view was a burning topical issue and is often referred to by Shakespeare. It is worth conjuring up these aspects of Elizabethan life if you are doing, for example, *Romeo and Juliet*, *Hamlet* or the *Henrys*. For an account of sword fighting in Shakespeare's time, see the relevant chapters in *Schools and Masters of Fence* by Egerton Castle (1892).

Shakespeare pandered less to his audience's taste for blood, encrusting poisons, amputations and lingering deaths than some of his fellow dramatists, although *Titus* and *3 Henry VI* are well stocked with horrors. Between *1 Henry VI* and *Lear*, violence in a sense withdraws from the physical arena into the minds of the protagonists. The more lifelike the plays became, the less convincing were the battle scenes; hence the Chorus' apology in *Henry V* for the 'ragged foils' and the 'brawl ridiculous'. Instead of struggling mutes and supernumeraries, other devices are used to suggest a battle. In *Henry V*, which is often thought of as an epic war play, actually the only violent event (except for one *excursion*: see below) is Williams hitting Fluellen with Henry's glove.

Your immediate problem is that unless your fights are thoroughly thought-out and practised they will be (a) dangerous to the actors and (b) embarrassing to watch. Remember that you are in competition with films, which convey the illusion of death in minute and graphic detail. In the theatre, where the audience knows that you, as the dead Hotspur, are about to get to your feet and bow, you will have to work hard to convince them of your wormy lifelessness. You will solve most problems by keeping your fights very simple and rehearsing them as often as feasible, and certainly before each performance. There must be no tentativeness or fumbling. Remember, too, that fights are highly charged emotional dramas in themselves and must be *acted*.

BATTLES

There is little evidence to show how battles were staged at the playhouses, other than the cryptic stage directions and Ben Jonson's disparaging description of actors who

> with three rustie swords,
> And help of some few foot-and-halfe-foote words,
> Fight over Yorke and Lancaster's long iarres:
> And in the tiring-house bring wounds to scarres.
> (Prol. *Everyman in his Humour* 1616)

One certainty is that there was plenty of noise, which would suggest martial happenings and also cover up deficiencies in the fighting area. *1 Hen VI* marks trumpet flourishes, drums, bangs, thunder, a funeral march, Talbot's horn, a peal of ordnance, a sennet and ubiquitous 'alarums'. There were probably other, uncued sounds such as shouts and groans, and no doubt tramping feet made a good noise on the boards. Guns, presumably firing blanks, and fireworks were used, and there was probably a back-stage cannon used for the peal of ordnance, and also the chambers that put an end to the first Globe. Perhaps the cannon made an occasional appearance; it would certainly have produced atmospheric smoke and smells.

Precisely what action is represented by the famous 'alarms and excursions' direction is not clear. An alarm may have been literally a cry or cries to arms, or general rhubarb by extras on or off stage. It seems also to indicate a signal given by trumpets or drums (especially when spelt 'alarum') or even a fast-beating bell, as in *Oth* 2.3. The word had begun to acquire its modern disembodied and emotional connotations:

A blanket in the alarm of fear caught up . . .   (*Ham* 2.2.540)

A few ad libs are marked, or implied. In *1 Hen VI* 2.1 the English cry 'St George' and 'a Talbot'; Hotspur's war-cry is 'Esperance', from the Percy family's motto. You could have the factions in *Rom & Jul* shouting their household's name, as in mediæval Italy they shouted 'Montecchi' and 'Capilletti'. If the cast are self-conscious about making war noises, remind them of football supporters and cheer leaders. Remember, though, that a cry to arms is a cry of fear, and should be chilling. Henry V's 'God for Harry! England and Saint George!' should raise the roof and the hair on the audience's head.

If you have a trumpeter/drummer in the company, you will be able to invent some exciting sounds (see p. 88–9). It is very helpful to have different sorts of sound for different factions: for example, you might use a drum for the Malcolm-Macduff army and a horn or pipes for Macbeth. In *Henry V* you could have a hysterical, high-pitched trumpet for the over-lusty French and a good honest drum for the English. For suppliers of battle noises, see below.

What about the 'excursions'? In military terms they are sorties, or raids. We do not know how the actors performed them. Most of them are marked in early plays: *Henry VI*, *Richard III*, *Henry V* and *Henry IV*. They may merely have consisted of hired men traversing the stage and bashing foils about and grunting, which is how they are usually performed still. It is difficult to make this sort of action look dangerous, and of course Shakespeare was aware of this. In *1 Henry IV* 1.3 there is a direction 'Excursions and Parties fighting' which implies that excursions were not actual fights. Perhaps they were in fact militarily executed sallies, bands of soldiers or single men rushing across the stage with weapons and colours, looking grim and purposeful. If you want to show Parties fighting, keep embattled groups *well apart*, and choreograph the movements as carefully as if you were staging Swan Lake. Remember that actors get excited in front of an audience and tend to spread out dangerously. However you do your excursions they must be quick and not hold up the story. They were intended, probably, to be impressionistic.

ARMOUR AND WEAPONS

Armour

Armour need not be a great problem. For practical purposes in the 1600s it was fast becoming obsolete, and the Elizabethan players probably made do with secondhand bits and pieces (see, however, the One in sumptuous armour, *Tr & Cr* 5.6.23). A few breastplates and helmets will convey a great deal. You don't want performers clanking about like the White Knight, and your audience almost certainly won't be expecting accuracy.

It is easier to use mediæval rather than Elizabethan designs for the history plays (Fig. 1). A jack, or padded shirt, worn over breeches or leggings, is a good all-purpose covering for all soldiers (Fig. 2). Lords and princes need at least a breastplate and helmet (Figs 3 and 4). You can fix gorgeous plumes on the helmet. Greeks and Romans *can* wear Renaissance armour, as in the Peacham sketch, but this may confuse your audience. Basic Greek and Roman shapes are illustrated in Figs 5 and 6. Chain mail can be knitted with string and sprayed or dyed silver. Colours, or banners, look marvellous on stage when flourished energetically. Pageantry and spectacle will compensate for any lack of authenticity. You can afford to go to town with gilt sprays and glitter, remembering the Field of the Cloth of Gold, *Hen VIII* 1.1.4.

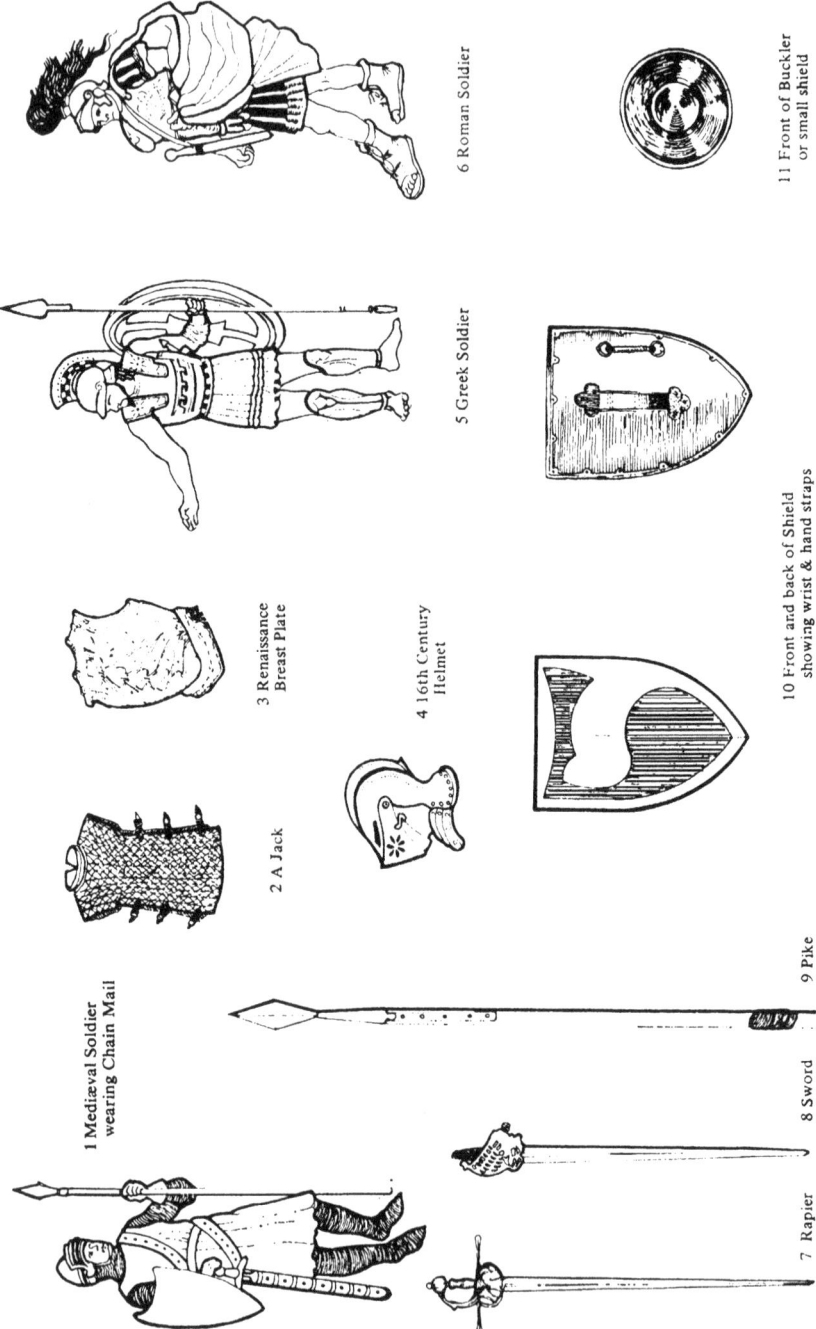

The Heraldry of Shakespeare by G C Rothery (Morland, 1930) will help with flags and emblems. Other book sources are given below.

Weapons

Soldiers can carry staves, bludgeons, pikes or pretty well anything. Higher ranks should have swords, although primitives like Douglas could invent their own personalized killing tools. There are not likely to be many experts on historical armaments in your audience. All fighters should carry shields. See Figs 8–11.

Here is a select list of suppliers. For others you should consult the *Amateur Stage Theatre Directory* (Stacey Publications, 1 Hawthorndene Road, Hayes, Bromley, Kent), which is published annually. You might also ask your nearest repertory theatre company for help.

Armour and Weapons

Bapty & Co Ltd, 703 Harrow Road, London NW10 (01-937 6671). Weapons.
Richard Dendy & Associates, 46 Sutton Lane, Banstead, Surrey (Burgh Heath 55733) Armour.
Paul Leon Equipment Co Ltd, 14 New N St, London WC1 (01-405 3832). Armour.
Royal Shakespeare Theatre, Stratford-on-Avon, Warwicks (0789 5920). Armour, chain mail, weapons.
Theatre Projects, 10 Long Acre, London WC2 (01-836 7877).
Theatreland Ltd, 14 Soho St, London W1 (01-437 2245). Chain mail.
Theatrescene Armoury Ltd, Suite 4, 12/13 Henrietta St, London WC2 (01-240 2116). Weapons.
Tony Watts, Farm Hill House, Dymock, Gloucestershire (240). Armour and weapons.
Robert White & Sons, 25 Shelton St, WC2 (01-240 3111). Armour and swords.

Noises, Smoke, Effects

Donmar Production Office, Albery Theatre, St Martin's Lane, London WC2 (01-240 1691). Optical effects, smoke guns, projectors.
L W Hunt Drum Co, 10/11 Archer St, London W1 (01-437 8911/3). Wind machines musical effects, drums, etc.
Stage Sound (London) Ltd, 14 Langley St, London WC2 (01-240 0955). Effects on disc or tape.
Theatre Projects.
Theatrescene Armoury Ltd.

Orson Welles' film *Chimes at Midnight* created a wonderfully realistic battle of Shrewsbury, fetlock-deep in churning mud. Though imaginative and helpful to the performer, this is not in fact the side of war that Shakespeare presents on stage, which is the glamorous, chivalric, poetic side, the propaganda of war:

> All furnish'd, all in arms,
> All plum'd like estridges that wing the wind,
> Baited like eagles having lately bath'd,
> Glittering in golden coats, like images,
> As full of spirit as the month of May,
> And gorgeous as the sun at midsummer...
>
> (*1 Hen IV* 4.1.97)

Even where the mud-and-blood side is talked of, it is coloured always by rhetoric:

> ...Dying like men, though buried in your dunghills,
> They shall be fam'd; for there the sun shall greet them,
> And draw their honours reeking up to heaven,
> Leaving their earthly parts to choke your clime...
>
> (*Hen V* 4.3.99)

One way of coping with battles is to stylize them. There are now established techniques for doing this: slow motion, masks, gigantic figures, strobe lights, dry ice or smoke guns and so on. The simpler your stylization the better. In a recent professional *Henry V* the battle of Agincourt was presented by a darkened smoky stage and huge and terrifying sound effects: whizzing arrows, neighs, rumblings, bangs and cries. Out of the gloom then reeled the unfortunate Le Fer with his captors, suitably muddy and bloody.

DUELS

If you do not have a fencer to arrange your fights, two helpful books on the subject are William Hobbs' *Technique of the Stage Fight* (Studio Vista, 1967) and *Weapons in the Theatre* by Arthur Wise (Longmans, 1968). Both these books describe a basic fight, with drawings. Sword fights in battles, such as Joan v Charles, Douglas v Blunt, Hotspur v Hal, Macduff v Macbeth, are best kept short and brutal with plenty of shouts and groans. Real swords which produce clangs and sparks are a help, but if you use mock swords remember to make them look weighty and to parry strokes as close to the hilt as possible.

Rapier or rapier-and-dagger duels (Hamlet/Laertes, Edmund/Edgar, Viola/Aguecheek, the *Romeo* fights, etc) need at least an elementary knowledge of fencing. The rapier is on the whole a young man's weapon in the plays; Shakespeare makes Mercutio scathing of Tybalt's newfangled Italianate style:

> **Mer.** He fights as you sing prick-song, keeps time, distance and proportion; rests me his minim rest, one, two, and the third in your bosom; the very butcher of a silk button... Ah! the immortal passado! the punto reverso! the hay!
> **Ben.** The what?

and Shallow (*Merry W* 2.1.232) says 'In these times you stand on distance, your passes, stoccadoes and I know not what; 'tis the heart, Master Page, 'tis here, 'tis here. I have seen the time with my long sword I would have made you four tall fellows skip like rats.' A stage direction assigns a rapier to Edmund (*Lear* 2.3.47); Kent, on the other hand, would use a sword.

Always bear in mind that there are members of the audience who don't know who is going to win. Notice how Shakespeare builds surprises into his duels. There are no straightforward fights to the death between Good and Bad: Macbeth, Edmund and Richard III all die unceremoniously in the tiring house. In the Hal/Hotspur fight an exquisite deflating commentary is provided in the Falstaff-Douglas side-show. In Hamlet v Laertes each kills and yet doesn't kill the other: they are both murdered by Claudio. In Mercutio v Tybalt there is the terrible irony of Romeo being the cause of Mercutio's death.

Always *act* your duel. A prime cause of unconvincing fights is that when actors are nervous they lose their stage characters and merely bang away at each other. Firmly establish the mental attitudes of the combatants and don't be afraid to introduce eccentricities or humour. You might have Hamlet, for example, very out of practise and sweating, and continually plopping down to catch his breath and limber up. In a recent production at Stratford, Mercutio treated his duel with Tybalt as a game, which he was reluctant to play, making mewling noises and rude schoolboy gestures. This worked very well. It will help if you concoct a psychological as well as a physical scenario.

BRAWLS AND MOBS

Romeo & Juliet, *2 Henry VI* and *Coriolanus* have important fighting crowd scenes. These can easily degenerate into an unconvincing, giggling mess, unless everyone is assigned short and definite actions. In real life, crowd skirmishes usually consist of a great deal of wary circling, followed by quick violent spats between two or three people. Protecting yourself, your eyes and head in particular, is as important as attacking. Cudgels of papier mâché or rubber are probably best for mobs.

A last word from Laurence Olivier:

> ... if you look as if you really *mean* it, and use carefully practised variation of rhythm, also with a few escapes—I mean purposely narrow escapes—some surprises here and there and a frill or two, your little fight can look quite respectable.
>
> (quoted from the Introduction to *Technique of the Stage Fight*)

7 Costumes and Props

How should you costume your play? At the Globe important actors seem to have worn their brilliant and expensive Sunday best (see pp. 26–7). Rank and file wore ordinary clothes probably of their own providing. Although historical costume was worn, a sense of historical accuracy was a thing of the future; a character such as Julius Caesar, who is described by Casca as wearing a doublet (1.2.267), would perhaps have sported some laurel leaves and an old-fashioned cloak as well, and thus appeared quite satisfyingly antique to his audience.

Since the Restoration there has been a tendency to use the plays as clothes-hangers, either (like Charles Kean in the nineteenth century) for the director to prove his erudition with 'accurate' sets and costumes; or (à la Irving and Beerbohm Tree) to create extravagant and astonishing spectacles; or, as in some modern productions, as a showcase for a designer or as scaffolding for a directorial concept. You may believe that by dressing your play in modern clothes, or by setting it in another country or century, you will draw attention to its universal relevance or to unexpected consonances. Or you may decide on an outlandish setting purely in order to astound your audience.

The obvious truth is that there is no *right* way to costume Shakespeare, any more than there is a right way to deliver the lines. The best costumes—like those worn in Granville-Barker's productions at the Savoy in 1912, for instance—will be beautiful to look at and comfortable to wear; and they will not distract from the play. Without any dogmatic intention, this chapter is based on the belief that an approximately contemporary style is the easiest means of pleasing, and not confusing, your audience, and of making your actors comfortable. Its other advantages are that (a) you obviate embarrassing clashes with the text (such as Cleopatra in pink leotards asking Charmian to cut her lace), and (b) you will be helping cast and audience to evoke the spirit of the original production; for all that *Julius Caesar* is set in ancient Rome, it is entirely a play of England *c* 1600. Its disadvantages are that (a) an historical wardrobe takes time to make and is expensive to hire, and (b) that the clothes tend to look like fancy dress and make actors feel stiff and artificial. Solutions to these problems are offered below.

For a Jacobethan production you will need the following basics for the men:

YOUTHS, NOBLEMEN, KINGS, MIDDLECLASS CITIZENS, ETC

(1) *Doublets and/or Jerkins*. There is not much visible difference between these. A doublet is a tight-fitting jacket and a jerkin is an over-jacket cut on the same lines. The jerkin can be of leather or some tougher material than the doublet; it can be sleeveless and open in front. With a sleeveless version you could wear a white shirt with or without ruffles. The doublet is closed (with buttons or hooks), can be pointed, shirted and padded in the stomach (peascod-bellied) or in the sleeves (See Figs 12 and 13).

With a doublet or jerkin you would wear:

(2) *Trunk Hose or Breeches*. Trunk hose were originally an all-in-one garment, consisting of enormous round padded 'shorts' attached to stockings (see Figs 14 and 15). (The word 'hose' could then mean either the trouser or the stocking section, or both; it could also mean breeches.) Actors are sometimes unhappy about wearing trunk hose, unless they have elegant legs like the youth in the Hilliard miniature. Trunk hose were gradually superseded during Shakespeare's lifetime by breeches, also known as Venetians, slops, gaskins (or galligaskins), which were looser and baggier than trunk hose. Breeches and hose were tied to the doublet with laces, called 'points', which were threaded through holes in the doublet lining. Hence,

    Clo ... I am resolved on two points ...
    Maria That if one break, the other will hold; or, if both break, your gaskins fall.

                                                      (*Twel N* 1.5)

Trunk hose often had canions, or knicker-like extensions down the thigh.

(3) *Gowns, Cloaks, Hats*. You wouldn't be seen in the street without a *gown* and a *cloak* or *hat* (see Figs 16–18). You kept your hat on indoors, even at meals, and doffed it only when you were

15 Breeches with Points, or laces

19 A Robe

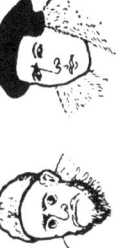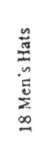

14 Hose with Canions

18 Men's Hats

13 A Doublet

17 A Short Cloak

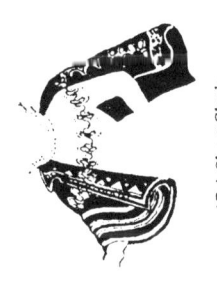

12 A Jerkin

16 A Gown with Fur Collar

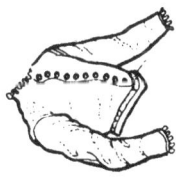

being particularly obsequious (eg to the Queen). Hamlet to Osric (*Ham* 5.2.96) 'Your bonnet to his right use; 'tis for the head;' and Touchstone very graciously to William (*AYL* 5.1.18): 'Cover thy head, cover thy head; nay, prithee be covered.'

OLDER MEN, MERCHANTS, COUNCILLORS, LAWYERS, DOCTORS, ETC

The versatile gown can be used for all these, with a *robe* for extra richness (see Fig 19). It can be homely black or brilliantly coloured, sleeved or not, fur lined, knee length or ankle length. See *Lear* 4.6.169:

> Through tattered clothes small vices do appear:
> Robes and furred gowns hide all...

CLERKS, SERVANTS AND RUSTICS

They can wear breeches either with a jerkin, in simple material, or with a shirt and cassock (see Figs 20 and 21).

ACCESSORIES

(1) *Boots and Shoes*. Shoes were worn by everyone except soldiers, hunters, travellers, etc, who wore boots. Hotspur, a horsey northerner, would be best in boots. Lear, who has been hunting, and Petruchio, an outdoor type, are both specified with boots. Shoes are often called pumps, and indeed they are rather like modern dancing shoes (see Fig 22).
(2) *Ruffs* can be made quite effectively from stiff interfacing (Fig 23).
(3) *Tippets*, or short shoulder-cloaks, give a weighty, rich look to a plain gown (Fig 24).
(4) *Gloves*. In leather, these would be practical for horsemen, soldiers, etc (cf Williams in *Hen V*), otherwise they were probably a mark of being well dressed, as in the nineteenth century. They have cuffs and may be embroidered.
(5) *Scarves and Handkerchiefs* of bright colours can be worn as mufflers or sashes, or across one shoulder. They were the mark of a military man, but were affected by fashionable youths. Lafeu says to Parolles (*All's Well* 2.3.202) 'the scarves and the bannerets

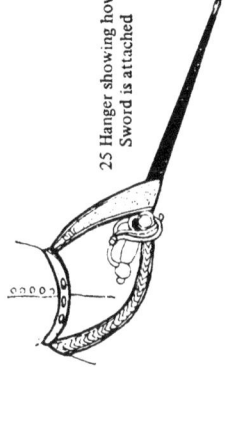
22 Boots and Shoes

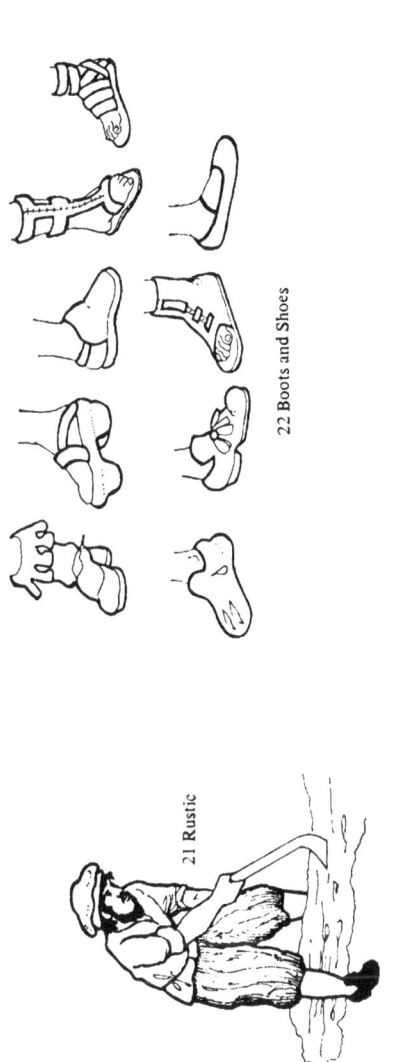
21 Rustic

20 Servant in Livery

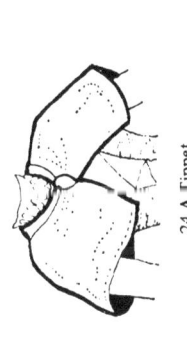
24 A Tippet

25 Hanger showing how Sword is attached

23 Ruff

about thee did manifoldly dissuade me from believing thee a vessel of too great a burthen.'

(6) *Codpieces*. In spite of the playwrights' fascination with them, these little embroidered and hinged boxes for enclosing the male genitals went out of fashion during the first half of Shakespeare's life. Eccentrics, like Pistol or Sir Andrew, might wear them.

(7) *Hangers* were for carrying swords, or possibly pen-cases, hunting horns, gourds or purses; your life might well depend on this part of your outfit (see Fig 25).

> **Osric** The carriages, sir, are the hangers.
> **Hamlet** The phrase would be more german to the matter, if we could carry cannon by our side.
>
> (*Ham* 5.2.164)

TOWNSWOMEN, NOBLE LADIES, PRINCESSES, ETC

(1) The basic *bodice* is a female version of the doublet, and will do for all kinds of women. For both doublets and bodices it is a good idea to copy the Elizabethans and have detachable sleeves, which can be swopped about. When Troilus gives his sleeve to Cressida, he would have to unhook or untie it at the shoulder, the fastening being concealed under the wings of his doublet (how Diomed attaches it to his helmet is a test of your ingenuity). The bodice can be separate from the skirt or not, whichever is easier (see Fig 26).

(2) *A Farthingale, or a plain skirt with petticoats*. The farthingale was the more fashionable garment; see Fig 27. A stiff hoop or hoops tied to the waist band with tapes will give you the right shape. The long pointed stomacher showed off your wasp waist, and could be spattered with jewels.

(3) A *gown*, or overdress could be worn on top of the bodice and loose skirt, for a rich, warm effect (see Fig 28).

(4) The *Smock* or *Chemise* was a linen shirt-like undergarment worn next to the skin. It had long sleeves, gathered at the wrists, to which ruffles could be attached. It also served as a nightdress.
Othello:
> O ill starr'd wench!
> Pale as thy smock . . .

(5) *Heads and hats* are very noticeable on stage. Women's hair was scraped back from the face, and mostly tucked under a cap or a hat (see Fig 29).

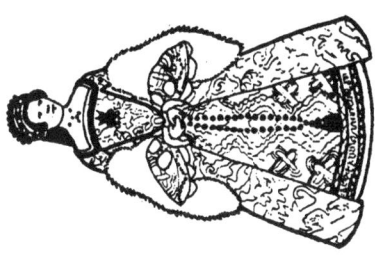

28 Gown with Fur Sleeves

30 A Countrywoman in Pattens

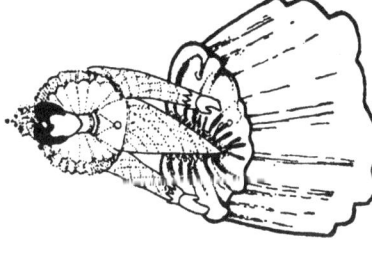

27 Lacy wearing a Ruff Stomacher and Farthingale Skirt

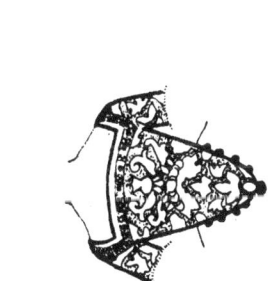

26 A Bodice

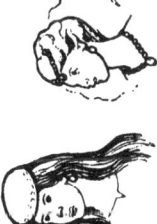

29 Hats and Head-dresses

COUNTRYWOMEN

A countrywoman would wear skimpy, plain versions of the skirt and bodice, with perhaps one petticoat and no farthingale. She could have pattens, and a cap or solid sort of hat (see Fig 30).

DECORATION

Both men's and women's clothes were elaborately ornamented and embroidered. You could use pinking, slashing, beading and interlining, and festoon the richer costumes with pearls and jewels; or simply use paint.

MAKING YOUR OWN WARDROBE

Clothes of between about 1570 and 1620 are not difficult to make. You can build up a wardrobe from a few basic patterns, using the cheapest, brightest materials you can find. The advantages of making your own wardrobe are that:
(a) The actors can choose what they want to wear (perhaps from looking at a selection of contemporary paintings). Thus, their clothes will fit and be flattering, and give them confidence. For school children, choosing the clothes could quite usefully develop into a fantasy in which you could discuss real or imagined materials, cuts and fashions (using information from the books listed below), remembering that ordering clothes was an important and expensive event to an ordinary Elizabethan. Or you could improvise on the Tailor scene from *Tam Shr* 4.3.
(b) It is more economical to make than to hire a wardrobe. An Elizabethan basic wardrobe is a good investment for schools and amateur groups. The basic bodice, breeches and most of the accessories can be adapted for other periods, or oversewn or dyed for your next Shakespeare production.

You may not be able to afford the silks, satins, taffetas, velvets, damasks and laces that the Elizabethan managers provided for their players, but you can achieve great richness with shiny cottons, linings and artificial fabrics. (See list of stockists below.) Here are some facts about colour which you may be able to use:
(a) In the sixteenth and seventeenth centuries, royal, navy or sky blue was worn by servants and apprentices, and the

tradition survives in the Bluecoat school uniform, and perhaps, faintly, in policemen's uniform. Blue-green, or popinjay blue, was popular among court ladies.

(b) Black and white are excellent stage colours (see *Oth* 5.2 and the stage direction for the Prince of Morocco in *Merch* V, 'A tawnie Moore all in white.') and both were fashionable in Shakespeare's time. Black was not particularly associated with mourning; it was both smart and respectable, and didn't show the dirt.

(c) Red and orange were popular colours. Red was conventionally the colour worn by lovers, unless they were in despair in which case they wore willow-green: 'Sing all a green willow must be my garland.'

(d) Yellow was the colour of fools; thus, Malvolio's yellow stockings, perhaps Sir Andrew's hair, Parolles' 'custard' or 'villainous saffron', etc.

If you can't afford either to hire or to make clothes, you could try for a 1600s 'look', using tights with puffy belted shirts, or long skirts over imitation farthingales made of thick material sausages. Beware of becoming too neutral and drab. Go for colours, especially in the comedies, and for making the actors look interesting and attractive, rather than designing an overall colour scheme. Part of the function of the clothes is to help the audience visually in their struggle with the foreign language. You can't be too blatant, for example, in differentiating the clothes of different factions, such as the Rebels and English in *Henry VI*, Volsci and Romans, town and country (in *AYL*) and so on. Shakespeare provides many opportunities for strong visual contrasts, and you should exploit them for all they're worth: Hamlet's inky black, for example, will only have its intended effect if the court is lightly and brightly dressed. Petruchio's and Grumio's provocative outfits work best when every one else is point devise, and so on.

WEARING THE CLOTHES

Clothes have never been so extravagant or so discussed as in the sixteenth century. Where we have only clothes or garments, the Elizabethans had habits, habiliments, caparisons, raiment, apparel, array, attires, weeds, robes, accoutrements and, a recently resurrected word, gear. Their quality was marked by their cut, as throughout the history of fashion, but equally by their ornamentation. Margaret in *Much Ado* praises the Duchess of Milan's gown for the complication of its trappings:

> ... cloth o'gold, and cuts, and laced with silver, set with pearls, down sleeves, side sleeves, and skirts round, underborne with a bluish tinsel ...
>
> (3.4)

Many of the inexplicable jokes in Shakespeare are to do with clothes. The precise flavour of these and countless other references is lost on us:

> **Lafeu** to Parolles: 'So, my good window of lattice, fare thee well: thy casement I need not open for I look through thee.'
>
> (*All's Well* 2.3.223)

And

> **Mercutio:** 'There's a french salutation to your French slop.'

In the portraits Elizabethan clothes look immensely uncomfortable by our standards: tight, bulky, scratchy, heavy and chilly around the legs. The whalebone or wire stiffening in doublets and bodices would have held you very upright, and given you a big-shouldered, curved-arm, broad-chested approach to life. The high collar or ruff would have made you keep your chin up proudly. Slouching and lolling would have been difficult, crossing your knees (in trunk hose) an impossibility.

But remember that portraits are fashion-plates, like the photographs in Vogue. They don't show you what people looked like as they went about their everyday life, or splashed through the streets on a wet winter evening. You are entitled to modify, since actors must be reasonably comfortable and they must feel and look real, not like dummies in a museum. Your audience won't be looking for textbook accuracy in the clothes; in fact, they won't know the difference between a slop and a strosser. As a director, you will achieve authenticity best by encouraging the actors to believe in their clothes rather than feeling that they're in fancy dress. You might do this in several ways:

(a) Provide the costumes, or a practice version, as soon as possible during rehearsals.
(b) Suggest that the cast describe the contents of their imaginary wardrobe, down to underwear and accessories.
(c) Discuss the differences between clothes then and now, and

their occasional parallels. Today, for instance, you can't instantly distinguish a doctor from a banker, as you could *c* 1600. The hose and codpiece drew attention to male nether regions, as do modern tight jeans.

(d) Discuss the social/practical/psychological reasons for the extravagances: the immense padding in the doublet, for example, may have had a protective function but it also made you more manly and impressive, like the rig of American footballers.

(e) Decide what fabrics you would use for your clothes if you were rich enough, where the fabrics would come from, etc. Think of how you would clean them, if at all.

(f) Encourage the actors to use personal, real details in their clothes, as well as in their accessories and props. Certain characters would be naturally untidy or dirty; Sir Toby might have a pipe and egg and ale stains down his doublet; Hamlet is clearly a slovenly sort of person (2.1.77–88); Brutus is vague (2.1.261). You can invent other sartorial eccentricities to help with characterization.

Without being stiff, try not to lose the essential big-chested upright feeling as you walk, sit, fight or dance. At the same time you should be light on your feet, remembering the light shoes and the fact that men were good walkers, riders and swordsmen, and that England—like ancient Crete—was famous for its dancers.

GREEK AND ROMAN COSTUMES

In spite of the night caps (1.2.245), the doublet (1.2.267), cloaks and hats (2.1.73), robe (2.2.107), mantle (2.2.192), it is usual to dress *Julius Caesar* and the other Roman plays in togas and stolas with tunics for soldiers and mechanicals. These sort of clothes may save trouble and won't baffle your audience; certainly, the stage blood soaking through Caesar's white and purple toga is always a success.

An indispensable source of Greek and Roman designs is M G Houston's book: *Greek, Roman and Byzantine Costume and Decoration* (2nd edition, A & C Black, 1947).

MEDIAEVAL COSTUME

This is often worn for the history plays, although not necessary. Historically, the period (*John c* 1160–1216, *Rich II* 1367–1400, *Hen IV* ditto, *Hen VI c* 1420–70, *Hen VIII c* 1490–1550) covers a huge range of styles, which you will find fully illustrated in:

C W and P E Cunnington, *Handbook of English Mediaeval Costume* (Faber, 1952)

Lucy Barton, *Historic Costume for the Stage* (A & C Black, 1937)

As with Elizabethan clothes, the less these feel like fancy dress to the actors, the better their effect will be.

Costume suppliers (other firms outside London are listed in the *Amateur Stage Theatre Directory*)

Morris Angel and Son Ltd, 119 Shaftesbury Avenue, London WC2 (01-836 5678).

B & H Costumes, 124 Wynchgate, London N21 (01-886 3173).

Bermans & Nathans Ltd, 3/13 Short's Gardens, London WC2 (01-836 3671).

A & L Corne Ltd, 3 Tanner St, London SE1 (01-407 3451). Headdresses.

C & W May Ltd, 9/11 Garrick St, London WC2 (01-836 5993) and Pantomime House, Oozells St, Birmingham 1 (021-643 6034).

Royal Shakespeare Theatre, Stratford-upon-Avon, Warwicks (0789 5920).

Fabric suppliers (to buy)

S. Borovick & Co, 16 Berwick St, London W1.

Empee Silk Fabrics Ltd, 39 Brick Lane, London E1 (01-247 1094).

M Klein, 2/4 Noel St, London W1. Trimmings, belts, buckles, etc.

J D McDougall Ltd, 64 Station Rd, London E7 (01-534 2921).

Theatreland Ltd, 14 Soho St, London W1 (01-437 2245). Fabrics, accessories, tights, etc.

FURNITURE, PROPS AND ACCESSORIES

Chapter 9 lists the props essential to each play. Further possibilities in terms of personal accessories and stage dressing are limitless; all depends on your funds and energies, and on the style you have chosen. If you have settled for the Jacobethan you will find the books listed below helpful. Remember Gremio's brochure of delights for Kate:

> ... my house within the city
> Is richly furnished with plate and gold:
> Basins and ewers to lave her dainty hands;
> My hangings all of Tyrian tapestry;
> In ivory coffers have I stuffed my crowns;
> In cypress chests my arras counterpoints,
> Costly apparel, tents and canopies,
> Fine linen, Turkey cushions boss'd with pearl,
> Valance of Venice gold in needle work,
> Pewter and brass, and all things that belong
> To house or housekeeping ...
>
> (*Tam Shr* 2.1.340)

Here is a select list of suppliers and reference books. Museums and country houses are also a fruitful source of information:

Suppliers (for a comprehensive list, see the *Amateur Stage Theatre Directory*)

Donmar Production Office, Albery Theatre, St Martin's Lane, WC2 (01-826 3221). Furniture for hire.

Dramaprops, 54 Aldermans Hill, London N13 (01-886 9842). Props for hire.

Eaves Handicrafts, 18a Slater St, Bold St, Liverpool 1. Do-it-Yourself costume jewellry.

Charles H Fox Ltd, 25 Shelton St, London WC2 (01-240 3111). Props for hire.

M. Harris & Sons, 44/52 New Oxford St, London WC1 (01-636 2121). Furniture.

Lewis and Kaye (Hire) Ltd, 1B Albemarle St, London W1 (01-493 5152). Silver and plate.

Midland Stage Decor, P M Pullon, 60 Engleton Road, Coventry, Warwicks. Props.

A Robinson & Son Ltd, 76 Neal St, London WC2 (01-240 0110). Props and jewellery.

Studio & TV Hire Ltd, Farm Lane, London SW6 (01-381 3511/2). Props, furniture and ornaments.

Useful books

M. Linthicum, *Costume in the Drama of Shakespeare and his Contemporaries* (OUP, 1936). A scholarly account of the fabrics, dress, colours, etc, referred to in the plays.

C Clark, *Shakespeare and Costume* (Mitre Press, 1937). Comprehensive and interesting.

M G Houston, *Ancient Greek, Roman and Byzantine Costume and Decoration* (2nd ed, A & C Black, 1947). Well illustrated.

C de Banke, *Shakespearean Stage Production* (Hutchinson, 1954). Drawings of furniture, props and costume details and discussion of fabrics.

H Melvill, *Historic Costume for the Amateur Theatre* and how to make it (Barrie & Rockliffe, 1961). Good Elizabethan section.

W Kenton, *Stage Properties and how to make them* (Studio Vista, 1964).

S Jackson, *Simple Stage Costumes and how to make them* (Studio Vista, 1968). Small section on Shakespeare, including how to make a ruff.

F M Kelly, *Shakespearian Costume for Stage and Screen*, revised by A Mansfield (A & C Black, 1970). The standard book.

J Arnold, *A Handbook of Costume* (Macmillan, 1973). A guide to the sources.

J Peters and A Sutcliffe, *Making Costumes for Plays* (Batsford, ed 1977). Many photographs of Shakespearian costume.

8 Music and Dancing

Try not to leave the music to the last minute. It should be as integral a part of your production as the acting, as real and as rooted in the text. Ideally your composer/musician(s) should be at all rehearsals, imbibing the spirit of the performance, perhaps improvising on the spot, as a trumpeter or lutenist might in actual life. If you have to use recorded music, rehearse with records or tapes from the beginning and encourage the cast to listen and make suggestions.

Obviously each play has its own musical needs, and the music you choose will be in the style of your production. The music of Shakespeare's own time is beautiful and—like the contemporary apparel—it is appropriate. The case for using the authentic Renaissance sound, or an imitation, is put persuasively by Ronald Watkins in *On Producing Shakespeare* (p 68):

> It is no mere archaistic affectation to stick to the period music... The overwhelming reason is that [Shakespeare's] was the golden age of English music, and that a strain of Byrd or Gibbons or Morley or Weelkes can evoke sooner even than Shakespeare's words the astonishing poetical freshness and vigour and strength of the age... anachronisms in musical texture are quicker than anything to destroy the sense of style.

No-one knows precisely who or what provided the music at the Globe or at Blackfriars. *Interludes and domestic music* such as Orsino's or Capulet's would probably have been played by a broken consort, which generally consisted of six players: lute, treble viol, bass viol, cittern, bandora and bass recorder. Morley's *Consort Lessons* (1599) were written for this combination. A modern equivalent to the broken consort would be guitar, violin, cello, harpsichord (playing both bandora and cittern parts) and alto flute. If using these instruments, you will need to write your own edition of whatever contemporary music you choose. A consort which is not broken is simply a string or wood wind ensemble, of viols, for instance, or recorders.

If your musical resources do not run to a consort, the next best sound is probably a harpsichord (playing off stage) or a lute, or failing these a six-string guitar. A lute is specified for Ophelia (in the Quarto) and the singer in *Hen VIII* (3.1), and could also be used by Feste, the boy in *Meas for M*, Lucius (*Jul C*), Balthasar in *Much Ado*, etc, or the songs may be unaccompanied. Though for the authentic sound a piano is a poor second to virginals or harpsichord, there are some good collections of Elizabethan keyboard music transcribed for piano (see book list below p. 91). The versatile violin is another possibility; it can be used for dances, song accompaniments or for effects such as the 'still and woful' music that brings Thaisa to life (*Per* 3.2).

Upper-class parties and banquets are often enlivened by hautboys, or oboes, because they make enough noise to oblige actors to raise their voices, and so convey a sense of crowded eventfulness. Hence they were also used for offstage effects such as the subterranean mystery sound in *Ant & Cl* 4.3. You could substitute bassoons, cor anglais, recorders or clarinets.

No written instrumental music for the plays has survived. You can either (a) adapt some of the works listed below; dance music can easily be used as interludes; you might launch *Twel N* out on a beautiful pavane, for instance; (b) brave the British Museum for other authentic sources; (c) compose your own neo-Elizabethan sound.

Processional and martial music cues are diligently marked in the text. The Flourish usually heralds the entrance of a sovereign or his representative, and might consist of two or three notes (although sometimes a 'long flourish' is indicated) played on a trumpet, or trumpets, cornets or sackbuts. A Tucket is a smaller sound, a sort of signature tune to announce the arrival of an important person. The Sennet was a longish cornet accompaniment to cover the entrance or exit of a procession. Trumpets, bugles or any combination of instruments with a brassy sound would be right for these signals. Battle signals such as the parley, charge, alarum and retreat, also played on trumpet or bugle, should be brief, nicely timed, exciting spatters. You will have to invent them, as there is no written music of this type. For ideas you might listen to the Marlowe Dramatic Society recordings of the plays (on ARGO-Decca). Marches and other drum signals can be played on a side or snare drum, muffled for funerals. A fife or pipe or piccolo or soprano recorder might accompany the drum. A pipe and tabor can be used for dances; and is also indicated for Ariel (3.2).

A few contemporary tunes for *the songs* have survived: Thomas Morley's 'It was a lover and his lass' (*AYL*), and 'O mistress mine' (*Twel N*); Robert Johnson's 'Where the bee sucks' and 'Full fathom five' (*Temp*); Thomas Ford's 'Sigh no more ladies' (*Much Ado*) and John Hilton's 'What shall he have' (*AYL*); John Wilson's 'Take oh take' (*Meas for M*), and 'Lawn as White' (*Wint T*); and Robert Jones' 'Farewell dear heart' (*Twel N*). Most of these and other songs either written or referred to by Shakespeare can be found in *Songs from Shakespeare's Plays and Popular Songs of Shakespeare's Time* (arranged for guitar) by T Kines (Music Sales Ltd, 1964). If you are not a stickler for authenticity, you could use an attractive setting by a later composer. Samuel French (26 Southampton Street, London WC2E 7JE) publish inexpensive collections of vocal music (including some instrumental music, notably for *Mids N*) by composers ranging from Purcell and Boyce to Arne and Mendelssohn.

If you are composing your own tunes make sure that you know exactly why the song is there, and be aware of its brevity and evocativeness. The words must be crystal clear. It is a good idea to allow whoever is singing to compose or discover their own version of their song(s), especially if the singing is characteristic, like Sir Toby's, or the Fool's in *Lear*, or the Gravedigger's.

Music cues are marked in the text more consistently than any other stage direction. This is not to say that Shakespeare did not want music at other points; some cues may have disappeared (Mardian may have had a song at *Ant & Cl* 2.5.123, for example). There were three trumpet calls to announce the beginning of a performance, the equivalent of the three knocks in the French theatre, or the three warnings over the tannoy today. There were dances at the end of a play and possibly a musical interval, but there is no evidence to suggest that incidental or mood music was played *during* a performance. If you want to elaborate or add cues—an interlude to cover a scene change, perhaps—be discreet. Remember to treat all music as part of the dialogue. The play musn't come to a halt while someone limbers up to sing a song. There should be no blank spaces. Tuckets and trumpet calls should be dramatic *interruptions*, and all highly charged martial sounds need to be topped by whoever speaks next. The playing, singing and dancing should be easy and unselfconscious.

DANCING

It is best to keep dances brief and like the fights they should be *acted*. Remind your company how important dancing was in the lives of all kinds of people; it was not only a pleasurable pastime, but an exercise and a skill and to some extent a ritual and a need. The origins of dances like the rondel and the morris lie in ancient fertility and sacrificial rites. The courtly dance in *Hen VIII* (1.4) should be a mating dance, not an anaemic waltz. The stage directions leave the choice of most dances up to you, but the possibilities are reviewed in detail by Cecile de Banke in Part IV of *Shakespearean Stage Production*. Steps of the galliard, lavolta, canary, branle and other dances are described, with suggested sources of music. Two other books which illustrate the steps in detail are:

T Arbeau, *Orchésography*. A sixteenth-century book of courtly dances, translated by C W Beaumont (C W Beaumont, 1925).

M Dolmetsch, *Dances of England and France from 1450–1600, with their Music and Authentic Manner of Performance* (Routledge & Keegan Paul, 1949). A comprehensive account with illustrations.

The library of the English Folk Dance and Song Society, Cecil Sharp House, 2 Regent's Park Road, London NW1 (01-485 2206) is another useful source.

BOOKS

An essential book for performers is *The Music in English Drama from Shakespeare to Purcell* by J S Manifold (Rockliff, 1956). This discusses instruments and types of music in detail.

E W Naylor, *Shakespeare and Music* (Dent, 1931 ed) has a chapter on dance.

New Oxford History of Music, Volume IV (OUP, 1968). This has sections on Renaissance instruments and notation, and on music in the drama, and has a good bibliography.

P J Seng, *Vocal Songs in the Plays of Shakespeare* (Harvard Univ Press, 1967). A scholarly book, with a bibliography.

F W Sternfeld, *Music in Shakespearian Tragedy* (Routledge & Kegan Paul, 1963) contains facsimile music, criticism and bibliography.

See also the chapter 'Shakespeare and music' by E J Dent in the 1934 *Companion to Shakespeare Studies*, and *Everyman's Companion to Shakespeare* (Dent, 1978) for short introductions to the subject.

PUBLISHED MUSIC

For songs

There is no comprehensive collection of song settings. A recent book is *Songs from Shakespeare's Plays and Popular Songs of Shakespeare's Time* (edited by T Kines) (Music Sales Ltd, 1964); this gives most of the authentic settings, arranged for voice and guitar.

W Chappell, *Popular Music of the Olden Time* (latest edition Dover, 1963). In 2 volumes, of which the first has a section on illustrating Shakespeare.

Some Shakespeare songs are included in *Forty Songs from Elizabethan and Jacobean Song Books* (4 vols), *Cavalier Songs 1625–1660*, and *Ayres, Songs and Dialogue* by Robert Johnson (all published by Stainer and Bell, 1976). Arrangements are for voice and keyboard.

For interludes and dances

Consort music

Music for Mixed Consort (Stainer & Bell, 1977). Has an informative introduction to the practical problems of performance, the instruments, and the use of improvisation.

Morley's Consort Lessons, reconstructed by S Beck (Peters, 1959).

Jacobean Consort Music (Stainer & Bell, 1962, in 6 parts). Arranged for early and modern string ensemble.

Keyboard and guitar music

Complete Keyboard Works, of Thomas Morley (Stainer & Bell, 2 vols).

Elizabethan Duets for 2 Guitars, edited by R Spencer (Stainer & Bell, 1973).

First, Second and Third Books of Aires, John Dowland (*1597–1603*) (Stainer & Bell, 1976, 3 books). Arranged for voice and keyboard, but includes lute tablature and bass viol part.

The Fitzwilliam Virginal Book (edited by J A Fuller Maitland and W Barclay Squire) (Dover, 1963, 2 vols). 300 airs with keyboard accompaniment.

My Ladye Nevell's Book of Virginal Music, William Boyd (Dover, 1969).

21 Masque Dances of the Early 17th Century for 1 Instrument and Continuo (London Pro Musica Edition, 1974).

Popular Music of the Olden Time, W Chappell (Dover, ed 1963) also contains dance music.

RECORDED MUSIC

It is only possible to give a brief selection from the wealth of contemporary music on record and tape. The current *Gramophone* Classical Catalogue should be consulted for other possibilities.

Records

Two Renaissance Dance Bands: director David Munrow. Includes dances for Broken Consort, by Morley (The Morley Consort): HQS1249. Also on tape: TC-EXE104.

An Evening of Elizabethan Music (2 records), consisting of Elizabethan Music (SER5687-8) and English Lute Music (SB2150), played by Julian Bream, with the Julian Bream Consort. Both records include dances.

Elizabethan Music, including dances and songs by Gibbons, Morley, Weelkes and others. The Purcell Consort with R Spencer on lute: ZRG652.

Orlando Gibbons. Church music played by the Jacobean Ensemble and sung by King's College Choir: ZK8. Also on tape: KZKC8.

Lachrimae, by Dowland. (Philomusica of London plays the famous pavanes and galliards.) OLS164.

London Early Music Group: interlude music by Byrd and his contemporaries: RL25110.

Music of the High Renaissance in England. The Purcell Consort of Voices and Jaye Consort of Viols playing Byrd, Morley, Gibbons and others. TV-34017S.

Shakespearian Music. A recital of early and modern music for the plays by the Praetorius Consort: REB191. Also on tape: RMC4023.

Shakespeare Songs. Sung by Alfred Deller with the Deller Consort; settings by Byrd, Weelkes, Morley and others: HMU202.

Tapes

Dowland, played by J Bream. Includes galliards and pavane music. RK11491.

Monteverdi's Contemporaries. Dances and Religious Music played by the Early Music Consort: TC-ASD3393.

Music for Elizabeth I. Played by the Purcell Consort, the London Sackbut Ensemble and the Elizabethan Consort of Viols: KZKC25.

Renaissance Suite. Includes branles and galliards played by the Early Music Consort: TC-HQS1415.

9 Performers' Guide to the Plays

This chapter is intended to guide your choice of play by indicating maximum and minimum casts, basic props and effects, and the very general problems involved in staging a full production. Most minimum casts can be made even smaller with the help of judicious cutting and adapting. Mute attendants, guards, soldiers, etc, have not been included in the casting since it is often possible to dispense with them (*Cor*, *Julius Caesar*, and the *Henry VI*s are obvious exceptions); otherwise, common sense will dictate which actors can be used as stage dressing. The comments are necessarily limited and subjective. For synopses of plots you could refer to the *Oxford Companion to English Literature* or to *Everyman's Companion to Shakespeare* (G and B Lloyd Evans, Dent, 1978).

A few general observations. In a contemporary production all men should wear swords or rapiers and/or carry daggers. Banquets do not demand papier mâché boars' heads, etc, merely wine, sweets and fruit. When lights are called for (eg *Ham* 3.2.285) they can be candelabra or electric torches disguised as flambeaux. Money is carried in leather draw-stringed purses, which can be attached to hangers (Fig 25). '*SSP*' refers to *Songs from Shakespeare's Plays and Popular Songs of Shakespeare's Time* by Tom Kines (1964).

ALL'S WELL THAT ENDS WELL

This 'rather nasty play', as the New Cambridge editor calls it, has embarrassed generations of Bardophiles. But it has possibilities. Think of it as a fairy story (reading the source is helpful; see *Arden* edition) and play it at a cracking pace, with plenty of business and atmospherics, spooky music, drums, cornets and colours. Cast your most beautiful and sexy actor as the awful Bertram. Trim the Clown and the funny bits. Beware of solemnity; scour the King, Lafeu and the Countess for humour. Find an outlandish style for the young men, with Parolles as its chief exponent. Helena, the most aggressive of Shakespeare's heroines, must be genuinely and wittily in love.

Casting: 16 male, 5 female, and mutes. Minimum cast: 10 males, 5 female, doubling thus: 1st Lord/1st Gent; 2nd Lord/2nd Gent; Page/Servant/Steward/Austringer; 1 soldier for all the soldiers; omit entrance of army and use anyone available for the noble bachelors (2.3).

Props: Ring. Letters. Handkerchief. Armour for Lords.

Music and effects: Flourishes, tucket, march and alarum. Music for Clown's song: *Was this fair face* (1.3).

ANTONY AND CLEOPATRA

A notoriously difficult play. Unless the principal roles are filled by actors with mammoth passions and galactic imaginations the play will not soar. The fourth and fifth acts are hard to focus, with their many tiny scenes and string of new and faceless characters. Very swift and basic staging is best, with flags and costumes to advertise each faction instantly. Octavius must have a steely glitter, to provide an interesting foil to Antony. Granville-Barker's *Preface* is illuminating.

Casting: there are speaking parts for at least 50 men and 4 women. The following can play mutes as well as the doubles suggested, to reduce the number of men to 17: Demetrius/Ventidius/Canidius/Servant 2.7; Philo/Silius/Taurus/Proculeius/Servant 2.7; Soothsayer/Schoolmaster/Clown; Messenger 1.2 and 1.4/Eros/Thidias; Messenger 1.2 and 1.4/Diomedes/Soldier; Messenger 1.2 and 2.5/Dolabella/Soldier; Lepidus/Sentry; Pompey/Scarus/Soldier; Menecretas/Decretas; Menas/Seleucus; Varrius/Gallus.

Props: Letters. Jewels. Knife (2.5). Banquet (2.7). Basket of figs and asps (5.2).

Music and effects: drums, trumpets, alarums, etc, for battle. Noise of a sea fight (3.10). Music for the banquet, possibly drums and trumpets at the end, with hautboys for musak. Music for the song: *Come thou monarch* (2.7). Hautboys under stage for 4.3.

AS YOU LIKE IT

An infallible play for young and old. The biggest acting burden is carried by Rosalind in the wooing scenes. It will help if the actress rehearses *as a boy*. Minor problems: the wrestling match, how to suggest the forest, the final dance.

Casting: 22 male, 4 female and Hymen (who can be either), plus extra lords. Minimum cast: 15 male, 4 female, doubling thus: Dennis/William; Charles/Martext/Jacques de Boys; Le Beau/Hymen; Lords in 2.2/Pages in 5.3.

Props: Chain (1.2). Table with food (2.7). Bloody napkin (4.3). Papers. Letter.

Music and songs: Music for the masque (perhaps flutes or recorders); music for final dance. Songs: *It was a lover and his lass* and *What shall he have that killed the deer* are both given in *SSP* with authentic tunes. There are also *Under the greenwood tree*, *Blow, blow thou winter wind*, *O sweet Oliver* and *Wedding is great Juno's crown*.

THE COMEDY OF ERRORS

This is the only play of which the original three-house staging is detectable, with one house for the priory, one for Antipholus' house and one for the Courtesan. Although often treated cavalierly by directors, it is an excellent little comedy, for young performers especially, and needs no addition or subtraction. The twins need only be vaguely alike, and should convey very different personalities. The play needs huge energy, knockabout business and broad characterization. Notice the unity of time and the clock references, reminding us of Egeon's doom. The dark undertones should not be ignored, and the more primitive humour—the servant-beating and Pinch-tormenting, for instance—should not be glossed over. The text is the shortest in the canon.

Casting: 14 male, 5 female, and extra citizens, officers, etc. Minimum cast: 10 male, 3 female, doubling thus: Duke/Balthasar; Jailor/Officer; 1st Merchant/Pinch; Angelo/Guard; 2nd Merchant/Messenger; Luce/Emilia.

Props: Money. Chain, bill, rope.

Music: no cues are marked, but you could invent freely: a town band, for instance, or exorcism music, or a nuns' chorus for 5.1. In a recent Royal Shakespeare Company production the play was turned into a musical.

CORIOLANUS

Shakespeare's most political play has attracted a small but devoted following in this century. It is crammed with interesting ideas and images, and needs a cast with a fairly mature understanding. Recent productions have tended to stress the politics at the expense of the sardonic comedy. It has various staging problems: the crowd scenes, the battle and fight in Act 1, what Dr Johnson calls 'too much bustle in the first act and too little in the last'. It is very long. None of the characters are particularly attractive, although Menenius, Volumnia, the Tribunes and Coriolanus are among the most interesting roles in the canon. The language is very compressed. Granville-Barker's *Preface* is indispensable.

Casting: This is definitely not a small-cast play. You need at least 2 separate crowds: plebs can turn into Roman soldiers (and back into plebs) and the Volscian army can double as Patricians/Senators. There are at least 33 male speaking parts and 4 women. Possible doubling: 1st Citizen/Lieutenant/Servant 4.5; 2nd Citizen/Servant 4.5/Soldier 1.10; Messengers 1.1 and 1.6/Aedile/Citizen 4.6; Titus Lartius/1st Watch; Senator 1.2/Herald/Citizen 2.3/Servant 4.5/Watch; Senator 1.2/Officer/Volsce 4.3/Citizen 4.6; Messengers 1.4, 2.1 and 5.4/Patrician/Citizen 4.6; Soldier 1.4/Officer/Patrician; Soldier 1.4/Citizen 2.3/Conspirator; 1st Roman/Citizen/Messenger 4.6/Conspirator; 2nd Roman/Citizens 2.3, 4.4, 4.6; 3rd Roman/Citizen/Messengers 2.6 and 5.4/Conspirator.

Props: Letters. Sewing (1.3). Spoils (1.4). Cushions (2.2). Dishes, etc (4.5).

Music and effects: Battle noises, drums, trumpets, etc. Fanfares for 1.10, 2.2, etc. Music for feast (3.5). Plenty of noise: 'The trumpets, sackbuts, psalteries, and fifes, Tabors, and cymbals, and the shouting Romans, Make the sun dance . . .'
Also: an Above and Within to suggest the walls and gates of Corioli.

CYMBELINE

This would be an adventurous choice. It is not the greatest of plays, but it is a good story, sometimes bizarre, sometimes spectacular, always quite funny and interesting. It is probably a response to the early Jacobean demand for romantic sagas. The compact narrative style is often clipped almost to telegraphese. Go for atmosphere, and realistic colouring for the characters, and don't worry about the plot's absurdities. The denouement is too long for modern tastes. The obsequies, battles and vision offer marvellous opportunities for imaginative staging. You need a cave for Belarius and sons.

Casting: In a full cast there are 22 male, 4 female and extras galore, plus musicians. By omitting musicians, dumbshows and 2nd Gaoler, and having very skimpy armies and attendants, the play will work with 16 male and 3 female, doubling thus: 1st Gent/ Dutchman/Messenger 2.1/Roman Captain/1st English Captain/ Ghost; 2nd Gent/Spaniard/Attendant 3.5/2nd English Captain/ Ghost; Pisanio/Jupiter; 1st Lord/1st Senator/Soothsayer; 2nd Lord/2nd Senator/Gaoler; Frenchman/Tribune/Lord 5.3/Messenger 5.4; Caius Lucius/Sicilius; Lady/Ghost.
Props: Ring, bracelet (1.2). Box of drugs, flowers (1.6). Letters. Bed, trunk, candle, book (2.1). Bows and arrows (3.3). Clothes, purses, dead game (3.6). Cloten's head, flowers (4.2). Bloody cloth (5.1). Chains, tablet (5.4). Armour and weapons.
Music and effects: Songs: *Hark hark the lark*, *Fear no more* (which may also be spoken); music from the 'ingenious instrument (4.2), probably an automatic organ, but any weird sound will do; solemn music for ghosts. Battle noises (4.4 and 5.2); thunder and lightning for Jove.

HAMLET

It is important not to gloom one's way through *Hamlet*. Use the energy of the play's humour to buoy up the bloodthirsty story and depressed hero. Don't spend precious time on the reams that have been written about the play, but concentrate on telling the story with pace and precision. Make the most of the Ghost, who is often the wrong sort of nonentity, and pay close attention to the Folio directions about sound and lighting. You need an arras for Polonius, a grave for Ophelia which might also be used for the Ghost, and a platform for the play and perhaps for the duel.
Casting: 32 male, 2 female. Minimum cast: about 15 male, 2 female, doubling thus: Bernardo/Player/2nd Gravedigger; Francisco/ player/Messenger 4.5; Marcellus/Player/Lord 5.2; Voltemand/

Fortinbras; Cornelius/Captain/Messenger 4.7/English Ambassador; Reynaldo/Attendant 4.6/Priest; 1st Player/1st Gravedigger; Boy Player/Osric/Sailor 4.6.

Props: Letters. Money. Books. Hamlet's gift (3.1). Skull, spade, coffin, flowers (5.1). Flagons, foils, jewel (5.2). Recorder (4.1).

Music and effects: Flourishes and cannon noise. Cock crow (1.1). Hautboys (3.2). Dead march. Songs: *How should I your true love know, Tomorrow is St Valentine's Day, And will he not come again* (versions in *SSP*), *For bonny sweet Robin, They bore him barefaced,* and the Gravedigger's *In youth when I did love (SSP)*.

HENRY IV PART I

The problem here is finding an actor large enough (in all senses) for Falstaff. Otherwise it is such a rich, funny, exciting play that you cannot go far wrong with it. The King must not be too fretful and dreary, or his scenes will sag. Hal works well if he is played very young and unwordly. The part of Hotspur is discussed in detail in Chapter 4. The tavern scenes must have tremendous reality. There are two duels and the battle of Shrewsbury, otherwise few staging problems. An arras is useful for both tavern and court.

Casting: 32 male, 3 female, plus mutes. Minimum cast: 15 male and 3 female (or 2 female if Lady Hotspur doubles with Mrs Quickly), omitting 4.4 and doubling thus: Westmoreland/Gadshill/Messenger 4.1; Northumberland/Vintner/Douglas/Sheriff; Blunt/Servant 2.3; 1st Carrier/Mortimer/Traveller/Messenger 5.2; Chamberlain/Francis/John of Lancaster.

Props: Letters. Money. Vizards (2.2). Wine jug and cups for tavern. Cushion/bill (2.4). Map (3.1). Bottle (5.3).

Music and effects: trumpets, drums, alarums, etc. Welsh song (3.1).

HENRY IV PART II

A less active and more autumnal play than Part I, but rich in its documentation of life as Shakespeare knew it. The Shallow scenes never fail, and Falstaff is funnier, nastier and generally more prominent. Pistol, so amusing to his first audience, is now an embarrassment; give him plenty of mad business.

Casting: about 44 male speaking parts and 4 female, plus attendants, soldiers, etc. Minimum cast 18 male, 4 female, doubling thus: Lord Bardolph/Bardolph; Porter/Fang/Drawer/Shadow/Beadle; Northumberland/Westmoreland; Travers/Drawer/Wart; Morton/Poins/Beadle; Servant 1.2/Francis/Mouldy; York/Warwick; Mowbray/Colevile/Groom; Hastings/Harcourt/Groom; Snare/Silence; Gower/Bullcalf/Gloucester; Poins/Feeble/Clarence; Peto/Prince John; Surrey/Davy/Messenger 4.1.

Props: Letters. Money. Flagons and cups for tavern. Crown. Dishes of apples and wine (5.3).

Music and effects: Sneak's noise (2.4), perhaps fiddles, or lute music. Music for King (4.5). Music for Silence's songs (5.3), and Pistol's warbles. Alarums, drums, trumpets, etc, for battle and procession.

HENRY V

Heroism and patriotism are out of fashion, and schoolboys are no longer required to memorize Henry's orations; but apart from this, it is a play that suffers somewhat from dearth of plot and thin characterization. Much depends on the magnetism of your Henry. Fluellen also needs strong playing. The French, as in *1 Henry VI*, should provoke jeers and catcalls. There is a dull patch towards the end of Act 4 before the grand finale of the wooing scene.

Casting: 38 male, 4 female, plus extras. Minimum cast: 17 male, 3 female, doubling thus: Hostess/Queen Isabel; Canterbury/French King/Williams; Ely/Constable; Gloucester/Governor of Harfleur; Bedford/MacMorris/Rambures; Clarence/Gower; Nym/York; Bardolph/Salisbury; Mountjoy/Burgundy; Boy/Messenger 3.7, 4.2; Cambridge/Fluellen; Grey/Dauphin.

Props: Treasure chest (1.2). Papers.

Effects: A suggestive cacophony for the battles: bangs, whizzes, trumpets, horses, etc; also flourishes, tuckets.

HENRY VI PARTS I, II AND III

The Henry VIs are a splendid means of introducing young people to Shakespeare and incidentally to a piece of English history. The drama is rude by the side of later plays (and is thus a useful critical touchstone); but if you latch on to the narrative thread, which is straightforward, and evoke the Elizabethan equivalent to the spirit of a spaghetti Western, everyone will enjoy themselves. It is vital that the cast should be clear about the historical facts. You could begin rehearsals by reading Hall's *Chronicle* (see *Arden* Appendix) and drawing up a large family tree to be kept permanently on view. For Part I you should have your audience booing and cheering at the fortunes of the French; clarify who is who with costumes and flags. It would be useful to have different trumpeters on stage to herald the entries of each faction. Part II is more subtly characterized, crueller and more eventful, and needs multitudes of energetic actors. Part III is crueller still, and noteworthy for the good roles of Margaret and emergent Richard III.

Casting for Part I: 37 male, 3 female, and extras. Minimum speaking parts: 27 male, 2 female. Unless you go all out for stylization you will need a crowd of mutes as soldiers, citizens, etc. Possible doubling: Countess/Margaret; Messenger 1.1/Servant 3.1/Shepherd; Messenger 1.1/Servant 3.1/French Sergeant; Messenger 1.1/Servant 3.1/Sentinel; Servant 1.3/Soldier/Porter; Mayor/Paris Governor; Officer/Falstaff; Master Gunner/Captain; Boy/Young Talbot/Messenger 1.3; Salisbury/Basset/Legate; Gargrave/French General/Scout; Glansdale/Lucy; Messenger 1.3/Servant 4.7/Keeper.

Props: Letters, pamphlets, etc. Roses (2.4). Torch (3.2). Coffin (1.1).

Music and effects: Alarums, flourishes, sennets, marches, etc. Thunder and lightning (1.4 and 5.3).

Joan must be a good swords-person. An Above is essential for Orleans and Rouen.

Casting Part II: There are over 60 speaking parts for men and 4 women. With doubling it can be done with about 28 men and 3 women: Beaufort/Iden; Messenger 1.2/Lieutenant/Herald/George; Hume/Master/Stanley/Messenger 4.7; Petitioner/Mate/Post/Soldier 4.6; Petitioner/Whitmore/Servant 2.4; Peter/Murderer/1st Citizen; Horner/Murderer/Richard; Hume/1st Gent; Bolingbroke/2nd Gent; Southwell/Messenger 4.4/Young Clifford; Spirit/Bevis/Messenger 4.4; One 2.1/Holland/Scales; Simpcox/Butcher; Mayor/Smith; Beadle/Cade; Neighbour/Clerk/Old Clifford; Neighbour/

Michael; Neighbour/Stafford; Prentice/Brother; Prentice/Lord Say/Messenger 4.9; Sheriff/Weaver/Edward; Mrs Simpcox/Eleanor.

Props: Papers. Bottles, mugs (2.3). Staffs and sandbags. Bed (3.2). Heads of Suffolk, Say and Cade.

Music and effects: Flourishes, sennets, battle sounds. Hautboys (1.1). Thunder, lightning, spirit effects (1.4). Sea fight, cannon (4.1).

Casting Part III: 48 male, 3 female, and extras. Minimum cast: 14 male, 3 female, omitting Pembroke, Bourbon, Stafford, running Falconbridge and Montague together, and doubling: York/Lewis/Stanley; Norfolk/Father/Somerset/Tutor; Clifford/Oxford; Northumberland/Keeper/Hastings; Westmoreland/Keeper/Rivers/Lieutenant/Montgomery; Exeter/Messenger/Post; Sir John Mortimer/Son/Messenger/Huntsman/Watch/Mayor; Sir Hugh/Post/Messenger/Watch; Rutland/Prince Edward/Watch.

Props: Somerset's head (1.1). Paper crown (1.4). Crossbows, prayerbook (3.1). Letters. Keys (4.7). Book, baby (5.6).

Music and effects: Flourishes, alarms, drums, march, etc.

HENRY VIII

Though well constructed, this play doesn't sparkle or resound. Without startling performances it can turn into a dull historical soap opera. However, it has at least the merit of unfamiliarity, and huge scope for pageant and crowds. Perhaps it needs a high-Victorian approach, with lofty sets, costumes all clinquant, plenty of atmosphere, swaying curtains, candles, slinky courtiers and smelly citizens, and all the bowing, trumpeting and ceremonial you can afford. Think of Holbein. Henry himself is a bland version of the bloated murderer of history, but some of the terror of Tudor despotism could permeate your production. It benefits from pruning, especially the slow-moving first act.

Casting: 35 male, 4 female, plus infinite extras. It would be eccentric to attempt the play with a small cast, but with threadbare processions and dances, and frantic costume changes, it can be done with 14 men and 3 ladies plus 2 mute ladies for Katherine's women/spirits/courtiers, etc. Doubling: Prologue/Epilogue/Vaux/Messenger; Norfolk/Denny; Buckingham/Griffiths/Porter; Abergavenny/

Campeius/Capucius; Secretary/Cranmer/Servant 1.4; Brandon/Cromwell; Sergeant/1st Gent/Keeper/Gardiner; Surveyor/2nd Gent/Butts; Chamberlain/Chancellor; Sands/3rd Gent; Lovell/Usher/Man; Guildford/Surrey/Canterbury; Anne/Boy; Old Lady/Patience.

Props: Banquet (1.4). Letter, book (2.2). Papers, letters, schedules. A ring.

Music and effects: At least 3 pieces of processional music are needed, on cornets, trumpets, drums, hautboys, etc. Music cues are clearly marked in the copious stage directions. Music for *Orpheus* (3.1), ghost dance and court dance.

KING JOHN

This play works very well with young people if it is simply staged, brilliantly costumed and not taken too seriously. The holes in the plot do not show when the playing is exuberant and the Elizabethan historical vision is well understood by everyone (the *Arden* has valuable information). It is not easy to act, and is thus a good exercise for student actors. Though much of the text is splendidly resonant, large and complex emotions are demanded without a supporting intensity in the language. Staging problems: the battles, and the Above for Angiers and for Arthur to leap from.

Casting: 26 male, 4 female, plus extras. Minimum cast: 14 male, 3 female, doubling thus: Essex/Executioner/Messenger 5.3/French Herald; Chatillon/Executioner/Peter; Robert/Lord/Bigot; Gurney/Lord/Melun; Arthur/Prince Henry; Austria/Messengers 4.2 and 5.5.

Props: Austria's head (3.2). Chair, irons, cord, paper (4.1). Crown.

Music and effects: Drums, trumpets, flourishes, battle noises.

JULIUS CAESAR

An astonishing mirror for whoever chooses to peer into it. Is it a play about public school virtues? Revolutionary austerity? A terrorists' apologia? Above all, it is a wonderfully theatrical and actable piece. Do not neglect any of the quasi-cinematic tension-building devices: the low drums, the taper, thunder, meteors, etc. A raised area is needed for the orations, the assassination and for 5.3.

Casting: 33 male, 2 female, plus extras. Minimum cast 20 male, 2 female. Unless you stylize your crowd, you need a number of plebs to become soldiers. Possible doubles: Flavius/Pindarus/Servant 3.1; Marullus/Messala/Servant 3.1; Octavius/Publius; Lepidus/Volumnius/Servant 2.2; Carpenter/Pleb/Soldier 5.4; Cobbler/Pleb/Soldier 5.4; Soothsayer/Cinna Poet/Poet 4.3; Cicero/Clitus/Servant 3.2; Casca/Strato; Decius/Varro; Cinna/Claudius; Metellus/Messenger 5.1; Trebonius/Titinius; Caius Ligarius/Young Cato.
Props: Letters. Pompey's statue. Wine and tapers (4.3). Orders (5.2). Ensign, laurel wreath (5.3).
Music and effects: Sennet, flourishes, drums, alarums. Thunder and lightning. Blood for Caesar. Lute and song for Lucius (4.3).

KING LEAR

It is sometimes said that *Lear* is unperformable, either because its agony is too terrible for the trivial atmosphere of the theatre, or because the part of Lear is beyond the scope of an actor. It is true that it is difficult to make madness and evil convincing on a stage, but it is not impossible. It is best to blot out all preconceptions and to base your thinking on the domestic core, as it were: the family relationships; and to find truthful bases for both the madness and the evil. Gloucester's blinding needs tactful staging. Don't let the tension slacken in the fifth act. The Edmund-Regan-Goneril triangle should be laden with sex and wolvishness, and they should have a horrifying sort of glamour. Granville-Barker's *Preface* is prescribed reading.

Casting: 27 male, 3 female, plus extra knights. Minimum cast: 11 male, 3 female, doubling thus: Albany/Servant 3.7; France/Curan/Gents 2.4 and 3.1/Servant 3.7/Messenger 4.2/Officer, Herald and Gent 5.3; Burgundy/Servant 3.7/Knight 1.4/Old Man/Doctor and Gent 4.7.

Props: Coronet, map (1.1). Money. Papers. Torches. Ring. Rope. A chain (4.2). A stocks for Kent (2.2).

Music and effects: Sennets, tuckets, flourishes, drums and alarums.

A dead march. Hunting horns (1.3). Storm effects (2.4 and 3.4). Tunes for Fool's songs (which may also be spoken).

LOVE'S LABOUR'S LOST

Inexperienced performers will have to work hard to capture the radiance of this play. Its action is nearly all in the words: in the wit of the clown, the boy and the ladies, in the poetry of Berowne and in the extravagances of Armado and the old men; so the text needs massive attention. An Arden edition is indispensable. You may want to trim the topicalities, and some of the humour. Differentiate the shapes and natures of the 4 lords and 4 ladies carefully, and beware of caricaturing the broad characters (Armado, Dull, Holofernes, Sir Nathaniel) beyond the bounds of reality. Because it is a masque-like play it has often been done with stylized settings and even with formal dance-like movements, but these do not help with the difficult text.

Casting: 13 male, 5 female, plus extras, or 12 male and 6 female if Moth is played by a girl. Minimum cast: 11 male, 4 female (or 10 male and 5 female), doubling thus: Ferdinand/Forester; Dull/1st Lord/Marcade; Jaquenetta/Maria. Omitting Blackamoors.

Props: schedules, scrolls, letters, pen, tablebook. Crossbows and arrows (4.1). Jewels, glove, pearl chain (5.2). 4 vizards, 4 masks (5.2).

Music and effects: Hunting noises off (4.1). Trumpet(s). Music for Blackamoors 5.2. Dances are sometimes added for the Blackamoors and/or disguised Lords, and also for the Worthies (5.2). Music for *Thou Canst Not Hit It* (4.1) (the original tune is given in *SSP*), for Moth's song (3.1) and for *When Daises Pied* (5.2).

MACBETH

The problem with the second half of this play is that the overthrow of Evil is less interesting, theatrically speaking, than the downfall of Good; and so it is important to make Macduff and Malcolm vigorous and interesting. Try to make the witches really frightening, rather than mere cartoon figures.

Casting: 35 male and about 7 female, plus mutes, lords, apparitions, etc. Minimally it needs about 16 men and 5 women, omitting

Hecate (who is superfluous) and doubling thus: Duncan/Old Man/ Caithness; Donalbain/English Doctor/Seyward; Captain/Messenger 1.5/Porter/Scottish Doctor; Angus/Messengers 4.2 and 5.5; Fleance/Boy/Young Seyward; 1st Murderer/Lord/Messenger 5.3; 2nd Murderer/Menteith; Lady Macduff/Gentlewoman. Seyton (notice his name) becomes a major-factotum chez the Macbeths. the apparitions are non-human.

Props: Letter (1.5). Torches, jewel (2.1). Daggers (2.2). Banquet (3.4). Taper (5.1). Branches, Macbeth's head (5.6).

Music and effects: Flourish, trumpets, drums, arches. Thunder and lightning for witches, Hautboys (1.5). Bell (2.2). Blood for hands. If Hecate is retained, songs and dances for witches (3.5 and 4.1).

MEASURE FOR MEASURE

An interesting play, which can be interpreted as you will. In essence it is a romance with a happy ending, but it raises and fails to resolve sombre issues. Death and despair are hovering presences. The humour is black or at best blue. Perhaps more than any other play, its success depends on the personality of its performers. The Duke, especially, as the puppet master, needs buoyancy and unexpectedness.

Casting: About 10 male and 5 female, plus mutes. Minimum cast: 12 male, 4 female, doubling: Francisca/Marina; 1st Gent/Servant 2.2/Abhorson; 2nd Gent/Servant 2.4/Barnardine; Friar Thomas/ Friar Peter; Elbow/Messenger 4.2/Attendant; Froth/Attendant. Varrius and the Justice are omitted.

Props: Letters, papers. Ragozine's head (4.3).

Music: Tune for *Take oh take those lips away* (4.1).

THE MERCHANT OF VENICE

Like the *Shrew* and *Othello*, this play raises an uncomfortable issue —in this case the treatment of Shylock—which must be discussed in its historical context by your company. It is a neat piece, but rather lustreless. Bassanio ranks in awfulness with Bertram, Claudio and Posthumus. Try not to make Antonio too depressing, nor Gratiano too tiresome. An Above is needed for Jessica.

Casting: 18 male, 3 female and mutes. Without mutes and with a rather empty court, male speaking parts can be reduced to 12, doubling thus: Morocco/Stephano/Jailer; Leonardo/Arragon/Duke; Old Gobbo/Tubal. All Portia's servants except Stephano are played by Balthasar.

Props: The caskets. Basket (2.2). Letters. Money. The Bond (4.1). Rings.

Music: Sennets. Music for *Tell me where is fancy bred* (3.2), and the 'house' music (5.1), which could be played by a consort.

THE MERRY WIVES OF WINDSOR

An enjoyable comedy for beginners. Most of it is in prose. Some of Ford's and Falstaff's speeches can be trimmed if necessary. The play must go at a gallop with all the hilarious business you dare to cram in. Beware of being earnestly humorous. Keep it light and warm and passionate, and rooted in real surroundings and feelings. Ford is a show-stealing part for a good manic actor. The last scene needs exciting choreography. The *Penguin* version has a good introduction.

Casting: 18 males, 4 females. Doubling is not possible without lethal cutting.

Props: Wine (1.1). Letters. Money. Box (1.4). Pen and paper (1.4). Mug for Falstaff. Book (3.1). Buck-basket big enough to hold Falstaff and foul linen, and portable on a pole. Cudgel (4.2). Lanterns for fairies (5.4). Buck's head, tapers (5.5).

Music and effects: Clock (3.2). Music for song: *Fie on sinful fantasy* (5.5), dance music and horns for 5.5.

A MIDSUMMER NIGHT'S DREAM

You cannot go wrong with this spell-weaving play. Beware only of allowing the lovers to be heavy; they should be hilarious. The fairies can be a directorial headache. Remember that in Shakespeare's time they were thought of as tiny (an agate stone on the forefinger of an alderman), and rather malignant. Granville-Barker's *Preface* is full of interesting ideas. Over-elaborate settings and costumes will destroy the play's delicate dream-like web.

Casting: 13 male, 4 female, plus at least 5 fairies (of either sex), attendants, etc. It is possible to double Puck with Philostrate, Theseus/Oberon and Titania/Hippolyta, as in the famous Peter Brook production. Otherwise Egeus can double as a Mechanical, and the Fairy in 2.1 can be one of Titania's four. This gives a minimum cast of 10 men and 3 women.

Props: Parts (2.1). Flower (2.2). Ass's head (3.1). Flowers (4.1).

Music and effects: Songs: *You spotted snakes* (2.2), *The ousel cock* (3.1). Music 'such as charmeth sleep' and dance 'to rock the ground' (4.1). Music for roundel (1.2). Music for 'Now until the break of day' and dance (5.1). Hunting horns and hounds (4.1). Mendelssohn is not only inappropriate but old hat.

MUCH ADO ABOUT NOTHING

The frothiest of Shakespeare's comedies, but worth doing for the Beatrice/Benedick and Dogberry/Verges scenes. It demands tremendous style and courtly sparkle, and absolute control of the verbal wit. Claudio and Hero need inspired invention. The vigorous sexuality of the dialogue should not be minced.

Casting: 20 male, 4 female, plus soldiers, servants, etc. If the Boy is omitted, and the Watch double with Messengers 1.1, 3.5 and 5.4, you need only 17 men.

Props: Masks (2.1). Pikes for the Watch. Stool, cushion (4.2). Arbour for garden scenes. Tapers.

Music: dance music (2.1). Music for *Pardon goddess of the night* (5.3) and the final dance (pipers are mentioned).

OTHELLO

You would not embark lightly on a production of *Othello*, although in the technical sense it has few problems. With its small cast and intense duologues, it is an ideal play for a small space. Iago should convince everyone on stage that he is honest. (see *New Penguin* text for a good discussion of Iago). Seize on Othello's exotic qualities, his way of speaking, for example. You need an Above for Brabantio, which can also be used in Cyprus.

Casting: 16 male, 3 female, plus extras. Minimum cast: 11 male,

3 female, doubling thus: Brabantio/Gratiano; Officer/1st Gent/ Herald; Duke/Gent; Senator/Lodovico; Senator/Montano; Sailor/ Clown; Messenger 1.3/Gent.

Props: Money. Letters. Wine (2.3). Handkerchief. Bed for Desdemona. Tapers and torches.

Music and effects: Storm (2.1). Trumpets and bell. Pipe music (3.1). Tunes for *And let me the canakin clink*, *King Stephen* (2.3) and the Willow Song (4.3) (see *SSP* for all three).

PERICLES

No one would claim that this is a brilliant play but it has an odd, ballad-like magic and is full of possibilities for an inventive company. The text is extremely patchy, so you can chop and adapt without conscience. The brothel scenes (once so shocking) are fairly innocuous in these gross times. The dumb shows can be omitted or turned into song-and-dance routines.

Casting: 39 male, 6 female and extras. Minimum cast: about 23 male, 4 female. Some possible doubling: Antiochus/Boult; Messenger 1.1/Marshal; Thaliard/Leonine; 1st Fisherman/Simonides; 2nd Fisherman/Philemon; 3rd Fisherman/Lysimachus; Dioniza/ Bawd; Lords 1.2/Sailors; Lords 2.2/Gents 3.2; Knights/Pirates; Lichorida/Diana.

Props: Net and armour (2.1). Shields (2.2). Baby (3.1). Chest, scroll, napkins, fire (3.2). Flowers (4.1).

Music and effects: Music for dances in 2.3. Magic for Thaisa (3.2). Marina's song (5.1). Storm (3.1). Antiochus' daughter's music (1.1).

RICHARD II

There is not much physical action in this sad and subtle play, and the actors need to be well in control of the richly poetic and political text. You need a startling Richard, and a good pulsing pace. Characterize the supporting cast strongly. An Above is required for Richard to descend like glistering Phaeton, and perhaps for 1.3.

Casting: About 36 male, 5 female, and extras. Minimum cast: 15

male, 2 female, doubling thus: John of Gaunt/Gardener; Mowbray/Fitzwater/Servant 2.2/Salisbury; Marshal/Abbot/Welsh Captain/Murderer; Aumerle/Berkeley; Bagot/Exton; Greene/Man/Keeper; Bushy/Man/Servant 5.4/Surrey; Ross/Groom/Lord 3.1/Herald; Willoughby/Murderer/Scroope/Herald; Duchess of Gloucester/Duchess of York/Lady.

Props: Regalia, mirror (4.1). Boots (5.1). Food (5.5).

Music and effects: trumpets, tuckets, drums, etc. Invisible music for 5.5.

RICHARD III

A good play for a large group. It calls for big acting, especially from the women, who should beware of being rhetorical and hollow. Overhanging canopies are enough to suggest the tents of 5.3. You need a throne for 4.1 and an Above for 3.7. Richard, everyone's favourite villain, obviously needs a quick-thinking witty actor.

Casting: About 45 speaking men and 5 women, plus mutes. Minimum cast: 25 men and 5 women, doubling as follows: Clarence/Bourchier; Lovel/Blunt; Brackenbury/Oxford; Gent 1.2/Richmond; Rivers/Messenger 4.4/Sheriff/Vaughan; Gray/Tyrrell/Brandon; Murderer/Mayor/Messenger 4.4/Surrey; Murderer/Messenger 2.4/Ely/Norfolk; King Edward/York; Citizen/Pursuivant/Scrivener/Ghost H IV; Citizen/Priest/Messenger/Herbert; Citizen/Messenger/Urswick/Ghost Edward; Boy/Page; Girl/Prince of Wales.

Props: Coffin. Warrant (2.3). Keys, fetters (1.4). Hastings' head (3.5). Clock, scroll (5.3).

Music and effects: Flourishes, sennet, drum, march, alarum.

ROMEO AND JULIET

The first part of the play, up to Mercutio's death, is swift, funny, violent; it contains 3 fights, a dance and the most famous love scene in the theatre. The second part is a downwards rush to the tomb. Until 4.3 the impetus is with Juliet, who needs great strength and energy. The lamentations of 4.5 are tricky. You need an Above, a bed and a tomb.

Casting: 24 male, 4 female, plus extras. Minimum cast: 12 male, 4 female, doubling thus: Prologue/Mercutio/Apothecary; Paris/Sampson/Guest/Musician; Gregory/Clown/Servant/Friar John/1st Watch; Abraham/Servant/Paris' Page; Balthasar/Servant; Benvolio/2nd Watch; Tybalt/3rd Watch; Montague/Capulet Uncle; Lady Montague/Guest.

Props: Letters. 2 phials. Masks (1.4). Basket (2.3). Logs and baskets, etc (4.4). Rope-ladder. Flowers, torches, mattock, wrench, spade, crowbar (5.3).

THE TAMING OF THE SHREW

Today the tormenting of Kate is not wholly amusing, whether or not you make Kate and Petruchio fall in love from the beginning —the romantic solution. But apart from this crucial problem, it is a very funny play with a curiously modern turn of phrase and joke, and fertile ground for the inventor of funny business.

Casting: If the Induction is retained, there are at least 27 male speaking parts (10 in the Induction) and 4 women. The Induction characters can of course turn into people in the play, eg Hostess/Widow; Sly/Pedant; Lord/Petruchio, etc. The number of Petruchio's servants is indefinite (at least 5) and they can be played by the rest of the cast.

Props: Mug, dishes, clothes, ewer, basin (Induction). Books, lute. Dishes, ewer, basin, etc, for 4.1. Gown and cap (4.3). Banquet (5.2).

Music: Flourishes. Horns. Tunes for Petruchio's snatches of song. Hortensio's fiddling (3.1).

THE TEMPEST

An oddly difficult play to bring off with an adult cast. However, its magicky, science fiction theatricality is in many ways well suited to children. Some understanding of its recondite themes is essential (the *Arden* will help). Music and effects need careful planning, and it is perhaps the only play where non-authentic music would not jar too dreadfully. A Within is useful for Caliban's den and the discovery in 5.1.

Casting: 14 male, 4 female. Doubling is not possible. Mute sailors can turn into Shapes, Reapers, Nymphs and dogs.

Props: Bundles of logs. Bottle (3.2). Banquet (3.3). Chess men (5.1).

Effects: Storm (1.1) and distantly in 2.2. There is no need for a ship. Thunder, lightning and the vanishing banquet (3.3) (see Appendix E in the *Arden*). Possibly, the descent of Juno; Confused noise and hunting noise (4.1).

Music: Strange, soft and solemn music is cued in the Folio. Dance music for reapers and nymphs. Pipe and tabor for Ariel (3.2). Songs: *Come unto these yellow sands, Full fathom five* (1.2), *While you here do snoring lie* (2.1), *Where the bee sucks* (5.1) (Ariel); *The master, the swabber* and *I shall no more to sea* (2.2) (see *SSP*) and *Flout 'em and scout 'em* (3.2) (Stephano); *No more dams* (2.2) (Caliban); *Honour, riches* (4.1) (Juno, Ceres). Music for masque.

TIMON OF ATHENS

'The castastrophe', says Dr Johnson, 'affords a very powerful warning against that ostentatious liberality which scatters bounty but confers no benefits.' The plot of *Timon* is as spare as a Greek tragedy, and it is a gloomy, rather unconvincing play without *coups de théâtre* or love interest, and so it is not often done. But it is useful for amateurs; it has many well-distributed parts and the text is not difficult. It needs clever handling to bring out its peculiar, almost surreal quality. Devise a plausible psychological casebook for Timon. The flattering lords need extravagant playing. Think of them as Jonson or Fellini characters. Use different coloured liveries to distinguish the servants, who are the real heroes of the play.

Casting: 37 male, 2 female, plus extras and Amazons. Minimum cast, without Amazons, 14 male, 2 female, with hectic doubling: Poet/Servant 1.2/Fool/Titus/Servant 4.2; Painter/Servants 1.2, 3.4/Varro Servant; Jeweller/1st Senator/Sempronius/Servant 3.1; Merchant/2nd Senator/Lucullus/Caphis; Messenger/Lord/Bandit/ Servant 3.1/Hortensius; Old Athenian/1st Lord/Lucius/Flaminius/ 4th Senator; Lucilius/2nd Lord/1st Stranger/Philotus/2nd Bandit; Lords 3.4/Stranger/Bandit/ 1st Lucius Servant; Ventidius/Servilius/Soldier/Isidore's Servant; Cupid/Page/Servant 2.2/Lord/ Senator.

Props: Jewel, picture, book (1.1). Banquets (1.2 and 3.6). Spade and gold coins in box (4.3).

Music: Trumpets, hautboys for banquets, music for masque and Amazon dance, drum and fife.

TITUS ANDRONICUS

Titus has been given such diverse labels as 'a Senecal exercise' and a 'heap of rubbish'. It is a cynical melodrama posing as a classical tragedy, and it can be quite horrible to watch. Your cast must consider why it was hugely popular in its time, by evoking its first audience's attitude to Roman history, for example, and its predilection for watching the torture of animals. The characters and atrocities must be taken seriously, and it needs big, passionate acting. The first act is surely corrupt, and you will have to rearrange or rewrite. A trap or pit of some kind is needed for 2.3, and your props department can be kept happy manufacturing hands, stumps, heads, pies, etc.

Casting: 20 male, 3 female, plus extras. It can be done minimally with 14 men and 2 female, plus at least 2 mutes, doubling thus: Bassianus/Goth/Judge; Captain/Publius/Judge; Tamora/Nurse; Alarbus/Young Lucius; Quintus/Clown; Martius/Aemilius; Mutius/Messenger/Goth/Judge.

Props: Coffin, palliament (1.1). Chest of gold (2.3). Napkin, knife, hand, 2 heads (3.1). Banquets (3.2 and 5.3). Books (4.1). Scroll, baby (4.2). Basket, money knife (4.3). Ladder, rope (5.1). Knife, basin (5.2). Bows and arrows with scrolls (4.3).

Effects: Drums, trumpets. Hunting noises (2.2).

TROILUS AND CRESSIDA

A rich play, but not an exhilarating one. The cynicism and sexuality translate easily into modern terms, and a mature group will respond to it well. Differentiate the Greeks and Trojans by costume and behaviour. Aeneas—Hector—Paris tend to blur together, and so do Agamemnon—Nestor. If possible, cast quite different physical types in the roles. Thersites is a problem. If he is too disgusting or monotonous he becomes tedious. He should find a real bitterness within himself, and perhaps play with a quiet venom.

Casting: 23 male, 4 female, and extras. Minimum cast: 16 male, 2 female, doubling thus: Alexander/Nestor; Helenus/Troilus' Boy; Menelaus/Paris' Servant; Priam/Calchas; Margarelon/Diomedes' Servant; Cressida/Cassandra; Helen/Andromache/Patroclus. Antenor is omitted and Deiphobus' lines in 4.1 and 4.4 are given to Paris' Servant and Paris respectively. The One and the Myrmidons can be played by whoever is free. The Prologue can be anyone.

Props: Letters. Torches. Book. Gloves.

Music and effects: Tuckets, sennet, alarums, trumpets and shouts. Tunes for *Love, love* (3.1) and *O heart* (4.4) (Pandarus). Broken music (a consort) for 3.1.

TWELFTH NIGHT

Like good wine, this play needs no bush, but it does need fresh and lively thinking. The Antonio—Sebastian scenes usually suffer from general indecision about Antonio's age, social class and sexual proclivities. Orsino should be steered towards eccentricity, rather than mere cheesecake sonority. Do not labour the play's autumnal, Chekovian qualities, which will emerge willy nilly if the acting is real and witty. A grilled trap door is effective as Malvolio's prison.

Casting: 15 male, 3 female. Minimum cast: 10 male, 3 female, if the officers double as sailors, Orsino attendants and servant 3.4; Curio as the Priest; Valentine as Fabian and the Captain as Antonio.

Props: Wine, cups, etc (2.3). Ring. Money. Letters. Gown and beard (4.2). Bandage for Andrew (5.1).

Music: Consort or lute music for Orsino. Tabor for Feste (3.1). Songs: *There dwelt a man in Babylon* (2.3), *When that I was* (5.1), *O Mistress Mine* (2.3), *Farewell dear heart* (2.3) and *Hey Robin* (4.2) are all illustrated in *SSP*. Other songs are *Three merry men, On the twelfth day of December* (2.3), *Come Away Death* (2.4), *I am gone sir* (4.2).

THE TWO GENTLEMEN OF VERONA

A slender courtly romance with robust undertones, excellent for beginners. The plot anomalies are perfectly acceptable in performance. Do not undervalue the vast amount of sexual innuendo in all its various guises.

Casting: 14 male, 3 female, plus extras. Minimum cast: 10 male, 3 female, doubling thus: Duke/Antonio; Eglamour/Speed; Host/Outlaw; Panthino/Outlaw; Sylvia/Lucetta; Launce/Outlaw. The Musicians play offstage.

Props: Letters, papers. Rings. Rope ladder. A dog (failing the genuine article).

Song: Who is Sylvia (4.2).

THE WINTER'S TALE

'This play... is, with all its absurdities, very entertaining.' Thus Dr Johnson, with his usual devastating encapsulation. After the absorbing first three acts, Shakespeare has thin and unlikely material to spin out, and the last two acts never quite grip in spite of Autolycus. Cast interesting, quirky actors as the young lovers, and keep the narrative humming along. Beware of sentimentality. Leontes is often too heavy, thus casting gloom over the whole play, but he should be funny and pitiful, closer to Ford than to Othello. The text of his scenes is quite hard to unravel.

Casting: 24 male, 8 female, plus dancers. Minimum cast: 9 male, 4 female, omitting Satyrs' dance, using the audience as the court (3.2) running together the parts of Servant, Attendant and 1st Lord in 2.3, having Emilia as the first Lady (2.1), and a thin rustic contingent, and doubling thus: Archidamus/Cleomenes/Shepherd; Camillo/Gaoler; Mamillius/Perdita; Polixenes/Officer; 1st Lady Emilia/Mopsa; 2nd Lady/Paulina/Dorcas; Lord/Servant 4.4; Gent/Mariner/Time; 2nd Servant/Clown; Antigonus/Autolycus; Dion/Florizel.

Props: Baby (2.3). Bundle of gold (3.3).

Music and effects: The storm. The Bear. Music for dances (4.3), and for Hermione's revival (5.3). Songs: *Jog on* (4.2), *Lawn as white* (4.3) and *When Daffodils* (4.2) are illustrated in *SSP*. Others: *Will you buy* and *Get you hence* (4.3) and *But shall I go mourn* (4.2).

Appendix

VOICE EXERCISES

Of course voice exercises are optional. There may not be time to do more than skim through this Appendix, and not a chance of inducing a cast—a class of scathing O-Levellers, perhaps—even to think about regular voice practice.

But the way you use your voice concerns not only how well you act Shakespeare; it is tied in with the way you think and feel, how relaxed you are, your energy level, your attitudes to people; broadly it could be said that your voice is an indicator of your attitude to life and therefore of life's attitude to you. Besides this, it is pleasurable to breathe correctly and speak with energy, in the same way that singing is enjoyable.

The phases of voice practice are logical: you first learn to locate and free all the muscles needed to produce your voice easily. These are the diaphragm, an umbrella-like muscle at the base of the lungs, the intercostal muscles and the muscles of the jaw, tongue and lips (see 1 below). You then learn to flex these muscles and tone them up with breathing and articulation exercises (2 and 3). Finally you should put everything into practice on bits of poetry and prose, and experiment with tone, volume and range (4).

1. Relaxation Exercises

(a) Lie down on your back on the floor. If it makes you more comfortable, put a book under your head to support it, and bend your knees up a little. Imagine you are a polythene bag full of water; you are heavy but buoyant; you tend to flow outwards; you would flow outwards forever if the walls of the bag didn't contain you. Feel the floor under your spine and shoulders. Try and release your thoughts and every muscle of your body. You are absolutely free.

(b) Tense your toes and squeeze them together; then let them relax. Tense your calf muscles and relax them; repeat with the muscles of your buttocks, stomach, shoulders, upper arms, lower arms and fingers, tensing and relaxing each in turn. Finally, tense the muscles of your face and jaw, and let them go. Let your jaw drop comfortably. Don't hurry. Roll your head gently from side to side. Imagine your neck as a lithe and supple stalk. Lie still for a while, enjoying the complete freedom of all your muscles.

(c) Put one hand on your stomach, at the centre base of your rib cage. Breathe in and sigh out deeply. You will feel a rise and fall under your hand; these are stomach muscles being moved by the action of your diaphragm, which contracts downwards to draw air into the lungs, like a pump. Now breathe in and feel the base of the rib cage move outwards with the help of the intercostal muscles. By exercising those muscles regularly you will increase your capacity for breathing from the base of your lungs, and add vastly to your vocal range.

(d) Breathe in and sigh out; you will hear a 'hrrrrrr' sound in your throat. Now try to breathe out without making any sound, staying quite relaxed. When there is no sound in your throat, it means that the air is flowing directly from your lungs to your mouth, with no tension anywhere in the larynx. This open, relaxed throat and unobstructed passage of air is what you should aim for when speaking.

(e) Try voicing little sounds: 'Ah', 'oo', 'er'. Don't use your throat but let the air from the lungs act by itself on the vocal cords. Say 'bah' quite loudly. Don't tense. You will feel your lips pressing together and exploding apart quite forcefully; they should tingle slightly. Your lip muscles are important because they frame certain vowels and form the consonants B, F, M, P, Q, V, and W. Now say 'lucky' several times quite fast and feel your tongue making the 'L' sound against the back of the top teeth, and the 'K' against the palate. Your tongue also makes D, J, G, N, R, S, T, X, Y and Z.

2. BREATHING EXERCISES

Breathe in slowly to a silent count of ten, feeling the base of the ribs expanding outwards and at the back as well. Breathe out to a count of 10 then 15, 20 and 25. Make sure you are always quite relaxed. Breathe in to a count of 3, and out to 10, 15, 20, etc.

Breathe in and count aloud as far as you can without strain. When you have run out of breath wait until you *have* to breathe in again, so that the rib muscles work eagerly and strongly.

3. ARTICULATION EXERCISES

Vowels should be open, which means that they are not held up by tension in the throat, or made nasal. Try saying 'oo' with a tight throat, and then a relaxed one. Practise the vowel sequence 'oo, oh, aw, ah, ay, ee'; think about the shape your lips make when you say these, and where your tongue is in your mouth. If you say them quickly, you will feel the middle of your tongue rising, and you will make a noise rather like a bottle filling with water.

Consonants are easiest to practise in pairs. Using the 'oo, oh, aw, ah, ay, ee' sequence, practise these groups, slowly at first, and then speeding up:

koogoo kohgoh kawgaw kahgah kaygay keegee
(tongue and palate)
looboo lohboh lawbaw lahbah laybay leebee (tongue and lips)
boodoo bohdoh bawdaw bahdah bayday beedee
(lips and tongue)
goopoo gohpoh gawpaw gahpah gaypay geepee
(palate and lips)
soomoo sohmoh sawmaw etc (tongue and lips)

The point of doing this is to strengthen the lip and tongue muscles which produce these sounds, so exaggerate each consonant slightly, feeling its muscular location in your mouth. The throat and jaw should always be relaxed. Think of the consonants and vowels as vibrating in your chest and facial cavities, which is where they resonate. Think of the consonants as bouncing outward, towards the listeners, with effortless energy.

4. TONE, VOLUME AND RANGE

(a) Stretch your arms up to one side, swing down to the floor and up to the other side, very loose and relaxed, speaking a poem or a piece of text as you swoop up and down. Or else jog and skip heavily around the room as you speak, remembering not to tense the throat. These exercises are recommended by Cicely Berry in her inspiring book *Voice and the Actor* (Harrap, 1973), to which Chapter 5 and this Appendix are much indebted. The physical action takes your mind off your voice and so releases it wonderfully.

(b) Sing your piece of text line by line on a single note, starting very quietly and gradually increasing the volume until you can't sing any louder without strain. Then speak the text: starting quite softly and increasing the volume line by line in the same way. Do not tense.

(c) Sing your text on one note, increasing the volume during the course of each sentence, and giving fullest weight to the last word. Speak the text in the same way. This is a very good exercise for the carrying-through of breath and thought: thus

> Two households, both alike in dignity,
> In fair Verona where we lay our *scene*,
> From ancient grudge, break to our new mutiny
> Where civil blood makes civil hands *unclean*.

(d) Say your text line by line, raising the pitch on each phrase. Don't let your voice go squeaky; change pitch *not* by tightening the throat, but by controlling the breath and relaxing your attack. You won't produce a good high note from a recorder if you blast away on it, and the same is true of your vocal cords.

Some good pieces of Shakespeare text for voice practice:

The Sonnets, especially XV, XIX, XXIX, LX and LXV. These are great tests for Shakespeare speakers, because they need lots of breath, vocal variation, energy and precision of thought.

The Choruses: *Henry V*, *Romeo and Juliet* and *Troilus*. These are written to be spoken fairly unemotionally; they are for conveying information, and must be extremely clear and interesting.

For breathing: Troilus (*T & C* 5.2.134–157)
  Cranmer (*H VIII* 5.5.15–26)
  Benedick (*Much Ado* 2.3.240–266) (prose)
  Lady Percy (*2 H IV* 2.3.9–45)
  Nurse (*Rom & Jul* 1.3.18–48) Men can use this too.
  Rosalind (*AYL* 5.2.33–46 and the Epilogue) (prose)

For rhythm: the Songs, especially *When icicles* from *LLL*, *Fear no more* from *Cymb* and *Blow, blow* from *AYL*.

www.ingramcontent.com/pod-product-compliance
Ingram Content Group UK Ltd.
Pitfield, Milton Keynes, MK11 3LW, UK
UKHW020857160426
5217IPUK00035B/1382